Wee...

FOR

Music Ministers

2014

Denise La Giglia

LTP

LITURGY
TRAINING
PUBLICATIONS

Nihil Obstat
Very Reverend Daniel A. Smilanic, JCD
Vicar for Canonical Services
Archdiocese of Chicago
April 16, 2013

Imprimatur
Reverend Monsignor John F. Canary, STL, DMIN
Vicar General
Archdiocese of Chicago
April 16, 2013

The *Nihil Obstat* and *Imprimatur* are declarations that the material is free from doctrinal or moral error and is granted permission to publish in accordance with c. 827. No legal responsibility is assumed by the grant of this permission. No implication is contained herein that those who have granted the *Nihil Obstat* or *Imprimatur* agree with the content, opinions, or statements expressed.

Author: Denise La Giglia

Special thanks to Deanne Tumpich and the music ministers at St. Julie Billiart Parish in Tinley Park, IL, for their generous guidance in the development of this resource.

Weekly Prayer for Music Ministers 2014 is based in part on the pattern established in *Children's Daily Prayer,* by Elizabeth McMahon Jeep.

As a publisher, LTP works toward responsible stewardship of the environment. Visit www.LTP.org/environment to learn more about how this book was printed.

WEEKLY PRAYER FOR MUSIC MINISTERS 2014 © 2013 Archdiocese of Chicago: Liturgy Training Publications, 3949 South Racine Avenue, Chicago, IL 60609. Phone 1-800-933-1800; fax 1-800-933-7094; email orders@ltp.org; website www.LTP.org. All rights reserved.

ISBN 978-1-61671-137-5

WPMM14

Lord God,

your beauty is ancient yet ever new,
your wisdom guides the world in right order,
and your goodness gives the world its
    variety and splendor.
The choirs of angels join together
to offer their praise by obeying your commands.
The galaxies sing your praises by the pattern
    of their movement
that follows your laws.
The voices of the redeemed join in a chorus
    of praise to your holiness
as they sing to you in mind and heart.
We your people, joyously gathered in this church,
wish to join our voices to the universal
    hymn of praise.
Grant that our ministry may be fruitful
and our worship pleasing in your sight.
We ask this through Christ our Lord.

(Prayer adapted from the *Book of Blessings*)

May the Lord be with you as you use your God-given gifts
in service of your parish. We thank you for your ministry.

Contents

Introduction

A cry from deep within our being, music is a way for God to lead us to the realm of higher things.[1] . . . Music is . . . a sign of God's love for us and of our love for him. . . . Singing together in church expresses so well the sacramental presence of God to his people.

—*Sing to the Lord: Music in Divine Worship*, 2

Music at church is about much more than entertaining an audience or showing off a skill. As the old adage sometimes attributed to St. Augustine goes, "When you sing, you pray twice." Song has been a vital part of the prayer of God's people for generations. You may remember some beautiful instances of song in the Scriptures, such as Mary's spontaneous song of praise to God (known as the *Magnificat*) upon finding out that she is pregnant with Jesus (Luke 1:46–55), or the angels appearing before the shepherds to announce Jesus's birth, singing "Glory to God in the highest," which we echo every time we sing the Gloria at Mass (Luke 2:13–14). When we gather for Mass each week, we raise our voices to sing God's praises and express our gratitude, just as our ancestors in faith did. When we sing God's praises together, we make God present to one another. The United States Catholic Bishops' document on music, *Sing to the Lord: Music in Divine Worship,* says, "God, the giver of song, is present

whenever his people sing his praises[2]" (1).

Music ministers serve an important role in helping to lead their communities in the sung prayer of the Church. It is important that music ministers prepare themselves musically, so that they can confidently lead the assembly in song and enrich the celebration through their musical artistry. It is also important that music ministers prepare themselves spiritually. *Sing to the Lord: Music in Divine Worship,* says: "Choir members, like all liturgical ministers, should exercise their ministry with evident faith and should participate in the entire liturgical celebration, recognizing that they are servants of the Liturgy and members of the gathered assembly" (32). So, it is important that music ministers prepare for the Mass prayerfully in order to fully exercise their ministry.

This resource contains prayers for every Sunday and Holyday of Obligation of the Church year, along with a few additional days when music ministers are likely to be gathering. Using the prayer for the coming Sunday during the week that leads up to it will help you to center yourself in the message of the Gospel and prepare yourself to worship more fully at Mass. You can use this resource in order to lead prayer at rehearsals or before Mass with a group, following the model below.

1. See St. Augustine, Epis. 161, *De origine aniemae hominis*, 1, 2; PL XXXIII, 725, as quoted in Pope Pius XII, Encyclical On Sacred Music (*Musicae Sacrae Disciplina*), no. 5.

2. Eph 1:1.

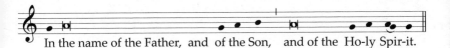

In the name of the Father, and of the Son, and of the Ho-ly Spir-it.

In the name of the Father, and of the Son, and of the Holy Spirit.

- **SIGN OF THE CROSS:** Pray the Sign of the Cross together in order to open and close prayer. If you like, you might choose to chant the Sign of the Cross as a group. The standard chant for the Sign of the Cross from *The Roman Missal* is above. You might also choose one of the other chant options from Appendix I of *The Roman Missal.*

- **PSALM RESPONSE:** Have the leader of prayer speak or sing the psalm response, and then have the rest of the group repeat the response. If you would like to sing the psalm response, you can use the response that your parish will be using for the coming Sunday. Depending on your parish practice, the words of the psalm response you will be using might be different from what is printed in the book. Just substitute whatever you will be singing for what is printed on the page. If you plan to chant the Sign of the Cross and sing the psalm response, you may want to leave a period of silence between the two, since the chant tones and the tune of the psalm response might sound jarring if done one right after the other.

- **GOSPEL READING:** You may want to invite someone other than the prayer leader to read the Gospel aloud.

- **SILENT REFLECTION:** Leave an ample period of quiet time after the Gospel reading so that everyone can reflect on the Word and read the reflection to themselves.

- **PRAYERS:** If you are praying with a group, you may want to select someone other than the prayer leader to read the intentions aloud. After each intention, have the group respond with the response given on the page. If your parish uses a sung response to the intentions, then you may want to substitute that sung response for what is printed on the page.

- **OUR FATHER:** Pray the Our Father together with your group. If your parish is accustomed to chanting the Our Father, then you may want to chant it.

- **CLOSING PRAYER:** You may want to have the prayer leader or another person read this aloud, or if you prefer, you can read it aloud together as a group. After the closing prayer, conclude in the same way that you began, with the prayer leader singing or speaking the psalm response and the group repeating it, followed by the Sign of the Cross (remember to leave some space between the two if you are singing/chanting both).

Advent

In the tender compassion of our God
the dawn from on high shall break upon us,
to shine on those who dwell in darkness
and the shadow of death,
and to guide our feet into the way of peace.

—Canticle of Zechariah

We call the days and nights before the Nativity of the Lord (Christmas) *Advent*, which means "coming." The Church reads and sings about God's promises. We tell the stories of many holy people: Mary and John the Baptist, Nicholas and Lucy. We strive for the time when God's love will be seen in all of us, when peace will come through people's acts of justice and love for each other. But, primarily, we wait. We wait for the blessed hope, the coming of our Savior, Jesus Christ, when all will be one, and the Kingdom of God will flourish. The Son of God already came to us, born in the city of David. This is what we celebrate at the Nativity of the Lord, and in Advent we ready ourselves and our hearts for his birth. We also wait for his coming again. We wait for his light to completely extinguish our darkness.

† *In the name of the Father, and of the Son, and of the Holy Spirit. Amen.*

Psalm
122:1–2, 3–4, 4–5, 6–7, 8–9

R. Let us go rejoicing to the house of the Lord. R/.

Gospel
Matthew 24:37–44

Jesus said to his disciples: "As it was in the days of Noah, so will it be at the coming of the Son of Man. In those days before the flood, they were eating and drinking, marrying and giving in marriage, up to the day that Noah entered the ark. They did not know until the flood came and carried them all away. So will it be also at the coming of the Son of Man. Two men will be out in the field; one will be taken, and one will be left. Two women will be grinding at the mill; one will be taken, and one will be left. Therefore, stay awake! For you do not know on which day the Lord will come. Be sure of this: if the master of the house had known the hour of night when the thief was coming, he would have stayed awake and not let his house be broken into. So too, you also must be prepared, for at an hour you do not expect, the Son of Man will come."

Silent Reflection

"Be prepared" is a key phrase in today's Gospel. It implies a mindfulness toward life, toward whatever it is we are doing in the present or however we choose to be in any moment. How else to prepare for an "hour [we] do not expect"? Mindfulness is a practice very much like preparing our music is a practice. Just as in our music-making we consider dynamics and breath, pitch and phrasing, so we need to pay attention each day to the way we treat one another and all of creation. Our song in the house of the Lord is magnified when we live it in everything.

Prayers
others may be added

At the beginning of this holy season of watching and waiting, we pray:

▪ **Come, Lord Jesus!**

Come, fill your Church with light and grace this Advent season, we pray: ▪ Come, and bring to the nations a true and lasting peace, we pray: ▪ Come, heal all those who are sick in mind, body, or spirit, we pray: ▪ Come, awaken us to the sound of your voice in the music of every moment, we pray: ▪

Our Father . . .

Come, Lord Jesus!
As we prepare our hearts for your coming during these holy days of Advent, open our eyes to recognize that you are already in our midst, in your Word, in the sacraments, and in all our brothers and sisters.
You live and reign for ever and ever. Amen.

Psalm
122:1–2, 3–4, 4–5, 6–7, 8–9

R. Let us go rejoicing to the house of the Lord. R/.

† *In the name of the Father, and of the Son, and of the Holy Spirit. Amen.*

December 8, 2013
Second Sunday of Advent

† In the name of the Father, and of the Son, and of the Holy Spirit. Amen.

Psalm   72:1–2, 7–8, 12–13, 17 (see 7)

R. Justice shall flourish in his time, and fullness of peace for ever. R/.

Gospel   Matthew 3:1–6

John the Baptist appeared, preaching in the desert of Judea and saying, "Repent, for the kingdom of heaven is at hand!" It was of him that the prophet Isaiah had spoken when he said: / *A voice of one crying out in the desert, / Prepare the way of the Lord, / make straight his paths.* / John wore clothing made of camel's hair and had a leather belt around his waist. His food was locusts and wild honey. At the time Jerusalem, all Judea, and the whole region around the Jordan were going out to him and were being baptized by him in the Jordan River as they acknowledged their sins.

Silent Reflection

What desire for release from the bindings of sin; what hope for freedom of spirit must have burned in the hearts of all those going out to be baptized by John in the River Jordan! Imagine the wonder of hearing John proclaim, "The kingdom of heaven is at hand!" Oh, that the lyrics of our melodies be such sweet blessing as this. St. Jerome urged singing not only with the voice, but also with the heart. When we discover the "kingdom of heaven at hand"

deep within ourselves, the song that comes forth will resonate with faith.

Prayers   others may be added

We hear the voice of the Baptist, and we say:

▪ **Come, Lord Jesus!**

That the Church may prepare the way of the Lord by faithfully preaching the Gospel of Jesus Christ, we pray: ▪ That we may prepare Christ's way in the world by working and striving after peace, we pray: ▪ That the poor may be blessed with God's gifts of joy, peace, and love, we pray: ▪ That our music may bring comfort to all those who are heavily burdened, we pray: ▪

Our Father . . .

Lord God,
the voice of the Baptist still resounds in the Church, calling us to repentance and transformation.
Teach us to live the Baptism we have received, and to prepare the way of the Lord until he comes.
Through Christ our Lord.
Amen.

Psalm   72:1–2, 7–8, 12–13, 17 (see 7)

R. Justice shall flourish in his time, and fullness of peace for ever. R/.

† In the name of the Father, and of the Son, and of the Holy Spirit. Amen.

December 15, 2013
Third Sunday of Advent

† In the name of the Father, and of the Son, and of the Holy Spirit. Amen.

Psalm *146:6–7, 8–9, 9–10 (see Isaiah 35:4)*
R. Lord, come and save us. R/.

Gospel *Matthew 11:2–6*
When John the Baptist heard in prison of the works of the Christ, he sent his disciples to Jesus with this question, "Are you the one who is to come, or should we look for another?" Jesus said to them in reply, "Go and tell John what you hear and see: the blind regain their sight, the lame walk, lepers are cleansed, the deaf hear, the dead are raised, and the poor have the good news proclaimed to them. And blessed is the one who takes no offense at me."

Silent Reflection
How does it feel to be reminded of our God's faithfulness in bringing healing to those afflicted and Good News to the poor through Jesus? Our music ministry is deepened when we stop and take in how God's way is revealed in lavish loving, and then reflect on how such love resounds in our own lives. The members of our assembly suffer from all manners of affliction, and often their troubles go unseen. Let our song be a compassionate gift of healing and a tender gift of gratitude for God's abundant love.

Prayers *others may be added*
To the One who fulfills all that the prophets foretold, we pray:

- **Come, Lord Jesus!**

That the Church may be filled with joy at the coming of the Lord: ▪ That all who do not have faith may know the joy that comes from faith, we pray: ▪ That those who suffer from depression and those filled with grief or anxiety may know light, hope, and peace, we pray: ▪ That our music may be refreshment for those who are bowed down in mind and body, we pray: ▪ That all our beloved dead may be brought into the everlasting joy of God's Kingdom, we pray: ▪

Our Father . . .

Lord our God,
may we rejoice in you always.
When doubts come, teach us to trust in your will, and to recognize that your Kingdom is coming even when we cannot see it.
Through Christ our Lord.
Amen.

Psalm *146:6–7, 8–9, 9–10 (see Isaiah 35:4)*
R. Lord, come and save us. R/.

† In the name of the Father, and of the Son, and of the Holy Spirit. Amen.

December 22, 2013
Fourth Sunday of Advent

† In the name of the Father, and of the Son, and of the Holy Spirit. Amen.

Psalm
24:1–2, 3–4, 5–6 (7c and 10b)

R. Let the Lord enter; he is king of glory. R/.

Gospel
Matthew 1:18–24

This is how the birth of Jesus Christ came about. When his mother Mary was betrothed to Joseph, but before they lived together, she was found with child through the Holy Spirit. Joseph her husband, since he was a righteous man, yet unwilling to expose her to shame, decided to divorce her quietly. Such was his intention when, behold, the angel of the Lord appeared to him in a dream and said, "Joseph, son of David, do not be afraid to take Mary your wife into your home. For it is through the Holy Spirit that this child has been conceived in her. She will bear a son and you are to name him Jesus, because he will save his people from their sins."

Silent Reflection

How often do we look to Joseph to remind us of what trust in God looks like? Like Joseph, we can choose to let go of confusion, fear, and doubt when they arise. We can listen for the song of hope God gives us in the other musicians who share our ministry. We can grow as a community, fostering friendship, love, and support. We can be the face of God for one another.

Prayers
others may be added

O Radiant Dawn, splendor of eternal light, sun of justice, we pray:

▪ **Come, Lord, and do not delay!**

That the Church, walking the path of penance and renewal, may grow in holiness, we pray: ▪ That the Holy Spirit may guide the nations into the path of peace, we pray: ▪ That all who are preparing to celebrate Christmas may be renewed in faith, we pray: ▪ That our music become an outward sign of the love we have for one another, we pray: ▪

Our Father . . .

Lord God,
give us Mary's faith, that we may believe in your promises.
Give us Mary's hope, that we may look to the future without fear.
Give us Mary's love, that we too may bring forth Christ by the love and kindness we show to others.
We ask this through Christ our Lord. Amen.

Psalm
24:1–2, 3–4, 5–6 (7c and 10b)

R. Let the Lord enter; he is king of glory. R/.

† In the name of the Father, and of the Son, and of the Holy Spirit. Amen.

Christmas Time

For, lo, the days are hastening on,
By prophets seen of old,
When with the ever circling years
Shall come the time foretold,
When peace shall over all the earth
Its ancient splendors fling,
And all the world give back the song
Which now the angels sing.

—"It Came upon the Midnight Clear" (CAROL)

On December 25, we proclaim, "*Today* is born our Savior, Christ the Lord." And so begins the celebration of the Lord's birth, of God becoming man. God loved us so much that he gave us his only Son to be one with us, to dwell among us, and to show us how to live in that love. He came to bring peace, to heal division, to end all pain, and to bring us into his eternal light. And so we celebrate the gift of his love. We fill the long darkness with beautiful lights. We sing carols and eat delicious food. Around the festive trees— trees right inside our houses!—we give one another gifts because God has given such good gifts to us, and we open our homes to guests because God has opened heaven to us.

December 25, 2013
Solemnity of the Nativity of the Lord (Christmas)

† *In the name of the Father, and of the Son, and of the Holy Spirit. Amen.*

Psalm
98:1, 2–3, 3–4, 5–6 (3c)

R. All the ends of the earth have seen the saving power of God. R/.

Gospel
John 1:1–5, 14

In the beginning was the Word, / and the Word was with God, and the Word was God. / He was in the beginning with God. / All things came to be through him, / and without him nothing came to be. / What came to be through him was life, / and this life was the light of the human race; / the light shines in the darkness, / and the darkness has not overcome it.

And the Word became flesh / and made his dwelling among us, / and we saw his glory, / the glory as of the Father's only Son, / full of grace and truth. /

Silent Reflection

So much practice has gone into preparing for the great feast of Christmas. Getting to rehearsals on winter nights is not always easy. Weather, traffic, work, and family demands can diminish your available time, not to mention the tug of making home preparations for Christmas. In the midst of so much busyness, what compels you to get to choir rehearsal? Consider this: You have been called by the same Word-made-flesh we celebrate on Christmas; you are called to shine the light of your song into the darkness of a broken world. Thanks be to God!

Prayers
others may be added

In the light of the Word made flesh, we pray:

▪ **Come, Lord Jesus, dwell with us.**

For all Christians, longing for the presence of the Savior, that we may be one: ▪ For all who do not believe in Christ, that they may find him by walking in integrity of heart: ▪ For children, especially those who lack the necessities of food, shelter, love, and hope: ▪ For the music-makers who lift heart and voice as witness to the light that no darkness can overcome, we pray: ▪

Our Father . . .

Lord Jesus Christ,
you are God from God, Light from Light,
*   Prince of Peace.*
Hear our prayers on this Christmas Day.
Forgive our sins, heal our divisions,
*   calm our fears; open our eyes*
*   to behold your Light, which no*
*   darkness can overcome.*
You live and reign for ever and ever.
Amen.

Psalm
98:1, 2–3, 3–4, 5–6 (3c)

R. All the ends of the earth have seen the saving power of God. R/.

† *In the name of the Father, and of the Son, and of the Holy Spirit. Amen.*

December 29, 2013

Feast of the Holy Family of Jesus, Mary, and Joseph

† *In the name of the Father, and of the Son, and of the Holy Spirit. Amen.*

Psalm
128:1–2, 3, 4–5 (see 1)

R. Blessed are those who fear the Lord and walk in his ways. R/.

Gospel
Matthew 2:19–23

When Herod had died, behold, the angel of the Lord appeared in a dream to Joseph in Egypt and said, "Rise, take the child and his mother and go to the land of Israel, for those who sought the child's life are dead." He rose, took the child and his mother, and went to the land of Israel. But when he heard that Archelaus was ruling over Judea in place of his father Herod, he was afraid to go back there. And because he had been warned in a dream, he departed for the region of Galilee. He went and dwelt in a town called Nazareth, so that what had been spoken through the prophets might be fulfilled, *He shall be called a Nazorean.*

Silent Reflection

In the news every day are stories of families who face challenges to their well-being. Natural disasters or personal conflicts can tear at the fabric of a promise to love and cherish forever. This Sunday's Gospel reminds us that even the Holy Family encountered unexpected difficulties, like upheaval and a concern over safety. There are families in your assembly who are weary and burdened over many things. Sing for them. May the sound of your song bring solace and comfort.

Prayers
others may be added

With Mary and Joseph, we pray:

▪ **Come, Lord Jesus, dwell with us.**

For the Church, that we may be one family, united in love, we pray: ▪ For refugee or migrant families, that they may have the strength they need, we pray: ▪ For families that are divided by distance or by discord, that they may come closer to one another in this holy season, we pray: ▪ For the families of our choir members and musicians, that they may face life's challenges with a spirit of trust, we pray: ▪

Our Father . . .

*Lord Jesus Christ,
you are the Lord of all, yet you chose to be born poor among the poor, the son of a simple family.
Teach us to love each other, to forgive each other, and to trust each other.
You live and reign for ever and ever. Amen.*

Psalm
128:1–2, 3, 4–5 (see 1)

R. Blessed are those who fear the Lord and walk in his ways. R/.

† *In the name of the Father, and of the Son, and of the Holy Spirit. Amen.*

† *In the name of the Father, and of the Son, and of the Holy Spirit. Amen.*

Psalm 67:2–3, 5, 6, 8 (2a)

R. May God bless us in his mercy. R/.

Gospel Luke 2:16–20

The shepherds went in haste to Bethlehem and found Mary and Joseph, and the infant lying in the manger. When they saw this, they made known the message that had been told them about this child. All who heard it were amazed by what had been told them by the shepherds. And Mary kept all these things, reflecting on them in her heart. Then the shepherds returned, glorifying and praising God for all they had heard and seen, just as it had been told to them.

Silent Reflection

What are the things you "keep" and reflect on in your heart as Mary "kept" what she heard about her child? What are the things that amaze you? How about some of the texts you sing? Do they ever take you by surprise or bring you to a new depth of understanding about life, love, and God's presence among us? As a new year begins, commit to noticing which texts draw you in, then take time to ponder and reflect on their meaning in your life. This is as important as learning to sing them well.

Prayers others may be added

As we celebrate Mary, the Mother of God, let us pray for peace, saying:

- **Prince of Peace, hear our prayer.**

For the Church, that we may be at peace, and strive to build peace, we pray: ▪ For the world, that this new year may mark the beginning of a new era of peace, we pray: ▪ For all who suffer the ravages of war, violence, or natural disasters, we pray: ▪ For all who glorify and praise God in song, that their prayer may resound in the hearts of all, we pray: ▪ For all mothers on this feast of Mary's motherhood, that they may love and cherish their children and lead them in ways of faith, we pray: ▪

Our Father . . .

Lord Jesus Christ,
Prince of Peace, hear our prayers on this
day of new beginnings.
With Mary's intercession to help us,
may we keep our resolutions to grow
in faith, to live in hope, to be active
in love, and to bring greater peace
to the world.
Who live and reign with God the Father in
the unity of the Holy Spirit, one God,
for ever and ever.
Amen.

Psalm 67:2–3, 5, 6, 8 (2a)

R. May God bless us in his mercy. R/.

† *In the name of the Father, and of the Son, and of the Holy Spirit. Amen.*

✝ *In the name of the Father, and of the Son, and of the Holy Spirit. Amen.*

Psalm 72:1–2, 7–8, 10–11, 12–13 (see 11)
R. Lord, every nation on earth will adore you. R/.

Gospel Matthew 2:1–2, 9–12

When Jesus was born in Bethlehem of Judea, in the days of King Herod, behold, magi from the east arrived in Jerusalem, saying, "Where is the newborn king of the Jews? We saw his star at its rising and have come to do him homage." . . . After their audience with the king they set out. And behold, the star that they had seen at its rising preceded them, until it came and stopped over the place where the child was. They were overjoyed at seeing the star, and on entering the house they saw the child with Mary his mother. They prostrated themselves and did him homage. Then they opened their treasures and offered him gifts of gold, frankincense, and myrrh. And having been warned in a dream not to return to Herod, they departed for their country by another way.

Silent Reflection

"'Tis a gift to come down where you ought to be," says the familiar Shaker hymn "Simple Gifts." In finding the child Jesus, the magi found themselves "in the place just right," to use another phrase from that hymn. And in this place that was "gift" to them, the magi themselves offered gifts to express their joy and gratitude. So do you. Within the liturgy, each voice in the choir, whether bass or alto, tenor or soprano, is a treasure, a gift offered freely, an homage given willingly. Each is important for the whole to "come 'round right."

Prayers others may be added

Christ the Savior has appeared, and so we pray:

▪ **Light of the nations, shine on us.**

That the Church may welcome people of every race, language, and way of life with understanding and respect, we pray: ▪ That Christ's light may shine on every nation, we pray: ▪ That we may welcome migrants, immigrants, and refugees with joy, recognizing the gifts they bring, we pray: ▪ That each choir member, cantor, and musician in the parish music ministry will cherish their special talent and continue to find joy in sharing it as gift to the community, we pray: ▪

Our Father . . .

*Lord Jesus Christ,
light of the nations, shine on us!
May your light so shine in our words and
actions, that others may be drawn to
you, and acknowledge you as Lord,
who live and reign for ever and ever.
Amen.*

Psalm 72:1–2, 7–8, 10–11, 12–13 (see 11)
R. Lord, every nation on earth will adore you. R/.

✝ *In the name of the Father, and of the Son, and of the Holy Spirit. Amen.*

† *In the name of the Father, and of the Son, and of the Holy Spirit. Amen.*

Psalm
29:1–2, 3–4, 3, 9–10 (11b)

R. The Lord will bless his people with peace. R/.

Gospel
Matthew 3:13–17

Jesus came from Galilee to John at the Jordan to be baptized by him. John tried to prevent him, saying, "I need to be baptized by you, and yet you are coming to me?" Jesus said to him in reply, "Allow it now, for thus it is fitting for us to fulfill all righteousness." Then he allowed him. After Jesus was baptized, he came up from the water and behold, the heavens were opened for him, and he saw the Spirit of God descending like a dove and coming upon him. And a voice came from the heavens, saying, "This is my beloved Son, with whom I am well pleased."

Silent Reflection

Resistance, confusion, questioning. All of this was going on inside of John, and yet he suspended all of it to respond to Jesus when he said, "Allow it now." Letting go of what makes the most sense isn't easy. We cannot usually see the outcome, or grasp the deeper "why" of it. We experience this tension in many of life's moments, even sometimes at choir rehearsal! Yet in letting go, John opened the way for the voice from heaven to reveal, "This is my beloved Son." Where in your life are you hearing, "Allow it now?"

Prayers
others may be added

Baptized in Christ, we pray in the Spirit:

▪ **Light of the nations, shine on us.**

That the Church may be continually baptized by the gifts of the Spirit, we pray: ▪ That all who are preparing for Baptism may be filled with Christ's light, we pray: ▪ That all who have died with Christ in Baptism may rise with him to new and everlasting life, we pray: ▪ That we who carry the song of our baptized brothers and sisters may have the courage to discern when to "allow" the confusing or unfamiliar for the sake of deeper knowing, we pray: ▪

Our Father . . .

*God our Father,
when we were baptized, the skies were not rent open, and no voice from heaven was heard, and yet we know that the Spirit descended upon us, and that your voice echoed in our hearts: "You are my beloved."
May we treasure our Baptism every day of our lives, and grow more and more in the likeness of Jesus Christ, your Son and our brother.
Through Christ our Lord.
Amen.*

Psalm
29:1–2, 3–4, 3, 9–10 (11b)

R. The Lord will bless his people with peace. R/.

† *In the name of the Father, and of the Son, and of the Holy Spirit. Amen.*

Ordinary Time
During Winter

I have waited, waited for the LORD,
and he stooped toward me
and heard my cry.
And he put a new song into my mouth,
a hymn to our God.

—Psalm 40:2, Responsorial Psalm for the
Second Sunday in Ordinary Time, Year A

For a few weeks in January and February, and then all through the summer and fall, the Church is in Ordinary Time. *Ordinary* comes from the word *ordinal*, which means "counted." In other words, each of the weeks has a number (for example, the *Third* Sunday in Ordinary Time). During this brief period of Ordinary Time between the end of Christmas Time and the beginning of Lent, we hear Scripture stories of the beginning of Jesus's public ministry and the call of the disciples.

January 19, 2014
Second Sunday in Ordinary Time

† *In the name of the Father, and of the Son, and of the Holy Spirit. Amen.*

Psalm
40:2, 4, 7–8, 8–9, 10 (8a, 9a)

R. Here am I, Lord; I come to do your will. R/.

Gospel
John 1:29–34

John the Baptist saw Jesus coming toward him and said, "Behold, the Lamb of God, who takes away the sin of the world. He is the one of whom I said, 'A man is coming after me who ranks ahead of me because he existed before me.' I did not know him, but the reason why I came baptizing with water was that he might be made known to Israel." John testified further, saying, "I saw the Spirit come down like a dove from heaven and remain upon him. I did not know him, but the one who sent me to baptize with water told me, 'On whomever you see the Spirit come down and remain, he is the one who will baptize with the Holy Spirit.' Now I have seen and testified that he is the Son of God."

Silent Reflection

We know that we give witness to our faith in the songs we sing during the liturgies at which we minister. How is that carried over into our lives? How do we make the way of Jesus known in our day-to-day living, in our relationships, or in our workplaces? Where do we testify in word or deed to the Spirit of Jesus among us and within us? How do others know of our conviction that we are all God's beloved? What we sing and witness to at liturgy must be lived daily.

Prayers
others may be added

To Jesus Christ, the Lamb of God who takes away the sins of the world, we pray:

▪ **Have mercy on us.**

For the Church, that we may celebrate the Supper of the Lamb with reverence and devotion, Lord, we pray: ▪ For all who feel burdened by sin, that they may turn to Christ, who takes away the sins of the world, Lord, we pray: ▪ For those who feel trapped in destructive habits, addictions, or relationships, that they may find freedom, Lord, we pray: ▪ For those of us who minister as pastoral singers and musicians, that we may discover and grow beyond whatever keeps us from more fully witnessing our "song," Lord, we pray: ▪ For all who have died, that they may come into God's presence with all of their sins forgiven, Lord, we pray: ▪

Our Father . . .

Lord Jesus Christ,
you are the Lamb of God, you are the
source of forgiveness, freedom,
and life.
May we turn to you at all times, trusting
in your mercy and love.
You who live and reign for ever and ever.
Amen.

Psalm
40:2, 4, 7–8, 8–9, 10 (8a, 9a)

R. Here am I, Lord; I come to do your will. R/.

† *In the name of the Father, and of the Son, and of the Holy Spirit. Amen.*

† *In the name of the Father, and of the Son, and of the Holy Spirit. Amen.*

Psalm   27:1, 4, 13–14 (1a)
R. The Lord is my light and my salvation. R/.

Gospel   Matthew 4:12–17

When Jesus heard that John had been arrested, he withdrew to Galilee. He left Nazareth and went to live in Capernaum by the sea, in the region of Zebulun and Naphtali, that what had been said through Isaiah the prophet might be fulfilled: / *Land of Zebulun and land of Naphtali, / the way to the sea, beyond the Jordan, / Galilee of the Gentiles, / the people who sit in darkness / have seen a great light, / on those dwelling in a land overshadowed by death light has arisen.* / From that time on, Jesus began to preach and say, "Repent, for the kingdom of heaven is at hand."

Silent Reflection

In the Gospel, we hear, "the people who sit in darkness have seen a great light," and "the Kingdom of heaven is at hand." This is wonderful news! Yet, Jesus also says, "Repent." This assumes a change, a turning, an expansion of our hearts. "I" must give way to "we," to the oneness of all in God. This challenges our egos; there is resistance. Consider how this is operative in you and do the inner work needed to move into the brightness of the light of God's Kingdom at hand. Then, in singing from

a place of your own transformation, you will invite the same from others.

Prayers   *others may be added*

To the Lord of every nation, we pray:

▪ Lord, hear our prayer.

For the Church, that we may bring the Gospel of Christ to every nation and every people, we pray: ▪ For outsiders, for all who feel rejected or ignored because of who they are, that they may find a welcome in the Church, we pray: ▪ For all who live in the shadow of war or violence, we pray: ▪ For each of us in the choir, that the words we sing may express the genuine and authentic resonance of a heart tuned to God's will, we pray: ▪ For all our beloved dead, that they may live in God's light for ever, we pray: ▪

Our Father . . .

Eternal God,
you are the Lord of every nation, and
your care extends to all who live.
Teach us to love all people as you
love them.
May we never allow prejudice or politics
to blind us to your presence in every
human person.
Through Christ our Lord.
Amen.

Psalm   27:1, 4, 13–14 (1a)
R. The Lord is my light and my salvation. R/.

† *In the name of the Father, and of the Son, and of the Holy Spirit. Amen.*

† In the name of the Father, and of the Son, and of the Holy Spirit. Amen.

Psalm
24:7, 8, 9, 10 (10b)

R. Who is this king of glory? It is the Lord! R/.

Gospel
Luke 2:36–40

There was a prophetess, Anna, the daughter of Phanuel, of the tribe of Asher. She was advanced in years, having lived seven years with her husband after her marriage, and then as a widow until she was eighty-four. She never left the temple, but worshiped night and day with fasting and prayer. And coming forward at that very time, she gave thanks to God and spoke about the child to all who were awaiting the redemption of Jerusalem.

When they had fulfilled all the prescriptions of the law of the Lord, they returned to Galilee, to their own town of Nazareth. The child grew and became strong, filled with wisdom; and the favor of God was upon him.

Silent Reflection

The old prophetess Anna beholds Jesus being presented in the Temple and knows him to be the one for "all who were awaiting the redemption of Jerusalem." She gives thanks for this hoped-for blessing. What might we take from this? Trust? Openness to mystery? Faithful discipleship? Even as we each ponder the meaning for ourselves, let us also collectively voice our gratitude to the elders in our choir for their wisdom, their presence, and their years of faithful ministry.

Prayers
others may be added

To Christ, the light of the nations, we pray:

▪ **Lord, may our eyes see your saving power.**

That all who have consecrated their lives to Christ may know his blessings, we pray: ▪ That Christ, the light of all nations, may bless the world with peace, we pray: ▪ That those in our music ministry blessed with age and experience may continue to live in the light of God's abundant love, we pray: ▪ That we may recognize Christ when he comes to us in the homeless, the abandoned, and the poor, we pray: ▪

Our Father . . .

Lord Jesus Christ, Light of the world,
may we who carry candles to honor
*   you today*
come one day to the light of your
*   eternal glory,*
where you live and reign with the Father,
in the unity of the Holy Spirit, one God,
for ever and ever.
Amen.

Psalm
24:7, 8, 9, 10 (10b)

R. Who is this king of glory? It is the Lord! R/.

† In the name of the Father, and of the Son, and of the Holy Spirit. Amen.

† *In the name of the Father, and of the Son, and of the Holy Spirit. Amen.*

Psalm
112:4–5, 6–7, 8–9 (4a)

R. The just man is a light in darkness to the upright. R/.

Gospel
Matthew 5:13–16

Jesus said to his disciples: "You are the salt of the earth. But if salt loses its taste, with what can it be seasoned? It is no longer good for anything but to be thrown out and trampled under-foot. You are the light of the world. A city set on a mountain cannot be hidden. Nor do they light a lamp and then put it under a bushel basket; it is set on a lampstand, where it gives light to all in the house. Just so, your light must shine before others, that they may see your good deeds, and glorify your heavenly Father."

Silent Reflection

In his homily one Sunday, a preacher asked, "Who fascinates you? Who do you want to emulate?" In the Gospel, Jesus is clear about what it means to be a person worth following: embody goodness and draw others to come into the light. What does that mean for you, specifically? What does being "light of the world" mean within your family, your neighborhood, your community, your parish, or your job? However you answer, this is the "you" brought to choir. This is the "you" who helps lead the assembly in song. Shine brightly!

Prayers
others may be added

Called to be salt and light, we pray:

▪ **Lord, hear our prayer.**

That the Church may be salt and light, shining forth in the world for all to see, we pray: ▪ That the world may know times of peace, we pray: ▪ That those who do not believe may encounter compelling examples of faith, we pray: ▪ That we who are the music-makers brighten our world and glorify God not only with our song, but also with the light of our good works, we pray: ▪

Our Father . . .

Lord our God,
Faith is a gift to be shared, not a secret
*   to be kept.*
Help us to be salt and light in the world
*   by living our faith with boldness.*
Through Christ our Lord.
Amen.

Psalm
112:4–5, 6–7, 8–9 (4a)

R. The just man is a light in darkness to the upright. R/.

† *In the name of the Father, and of the Son, and of the Holy Spirit. Amen.*

† *In the name of the Father, and of the Son, and of the Holy Spirit. Amen.*

Psalm   *119:1–2, 4–5, 17–18, 33–34 (1b)*

R. Blessed are they who follow the law of the Lord! R/.

Gospel   *Matthew 5:17–37*

Jesus said to his disciples: "Do not think that I have come to abolish the law or the prophets. I have come not to abolish but to fulfill. Amen, I say to you, until heaven and earth pass away, not the smallest letter or the smallest part of a letter will pass from the law, until all things have taken place. Therefore, whoever breaks one of the least of these commandments and teaches others to do so will be called least in the kingdom of heaven. But whoever obeys and teaches these commandments will be called greatest in the kingdom of heaven."

Silent Reflection

Music has its basic rules. It is written in a framework of meter, key, and tempo. A director brings music to life not only by honoring this framework, but also by inviting close attention to the pitch, dynamics, phrasing, and even the stillness of the rests. Jesus reminds us that the laws and commandments are important, yet are given breadth by how they are fulfilled—in a spirit of loving obedience and with a desire to pass them on to others. In both life and music, the art is in moving from a "head" approach to a "heart" approach.

Prayers   *others may be added*

To the Lord who gives us the great commandment of love, let us pray, saying:

▪ **Lord, graciously hear us.**

That the Church may preach and live Christ's radical Gospel of love, we pray: ▪ That the nations may be reconciled and live at peace with one another, we pray: ▪ That we may seek reconciliation with those we have wronged, and those who have wronged us, we pray: ▪ That within the boundaries placed on both our lives and our music-making, we be expansive, generous, and intentional, we pray: ▪

Our Father . . .

God of forgiveness,
help us to let go of grudges, to forgive those who have wronged us, to seek forgiveness for the wrong we have done, and so come to your altar in perfect freedom.
Through Christ our Lord.
Amen.

Psalm   *119:1–2, 4–5, 17–18, 33–34 (1b)*

R. Blessed are they who follow the law of the Lord! R/.

† *In the name of the Father, and of the Son, and of the Holy Spirit. Amen.*

February 23, 2014
Seventh Sunday in Ordinary Time

† *In the name of the Father, and of the Son, and of the Holy Spirit. Amen.*

Psalm
103:1–2, 3–4, 8, 10, 12–13 (8a)

R. The Lord is kind and merciful. R/.

Gospel
Matthew 5:38, 43–48

Jesus said to his disciples: "You have heard that it was said, *You shall love your neighbor and hate your enemy.* But I say to you, love your enemies and pray for those who persecute you, that you may be children of your heavenly Father, for he makes his sun rise on the bad and the good, and causes rain to fall on the just and the unjust. For if you love those who love you, what recompense will you have? Do not the tax collectors do the same? And if you greet your brothers only, what is unusual about that? Do not the pagans do the same? So be perfect, just as your heavenly Father is perfect."

Silent Reflection

Jesus gives us a template for loving, for a way of being, that is still so radical. Unconditional loving as synonymous with perfection can seem out of our grasp. Yet, consider how we approach our music-making. We strive for the perfection of it and give our best effort, but there is always something more to improve. Can we ever be perfect? Rather, in any given moment, we can be excellent. Perhaps the process is as important as the goal. Be excellent in loving in any one moment, and strive for even more in the next moment, and the next, and the next . . .

Prayers
others may be added

To God, who calls us to be instruments of peace in the world, let us pray, saying:

▪ **Lord, hear our prayer.**

For peace in the Church, we pray: ▪
For peace in the world, we pray: ▪
For peace in our families, we pray: ▪
For peace among our choir members, we pray: ▪

Our Father . . .

Lord,
make us instruments of your peace.
Where there is hatred, let us sow love;
where there is injury, pardon;
where there is doubt, faith;
where there is despair, hope;
where there is darkness, light;
and where there is sadness, joy.
Through Christ our Lord.
Amen.

Psalm
103:1–2, 3–4, 8, 10, 12–13 (8a)

R. The Lord is kind and merciful. R/.

† *In the name of the Father, and of the Son, and of the Holy Spirit. Amen.*

† *In the name of the Father, and of the Son, and of the Holy Spirit. Amen.*

Psalm
62:2–3, 6–7, 8–9 (6a)

R. Rest in God alone, my soul. R/.

Gospel
Matthew 6:24–30

Jesus said to his disciples: "No one can serve two masters. He will either hate one and love the other, or be devoted to one and despise the other. You cannot serve God and mammon.

"Therefore I tell you, do not worry about your life, what you will eat or drink, or about your body, what you will wear. Is not life more than food and the body more than clothing? Look at the birds in the sky; they do not sow or reap, they gather nothing into barns, yet your heavenly Father feeds them. Are not you more important than they? Can any of you by worrying add a single moment to your life-span? Why are you anxious about clothes? Learn from the way the wild flowers grow. They do not work or spin. But I tell you that not even Solomon in all his splendor was clothed like one of them. If God so clothes the grass of the field, which grows today and is thrown into the oven tomorrow, will he not much more provide for you, O you of little faith?"

Silent Reflection

Worry and anxiety are feelings that can sap our energies and distract us from the fullness of living. Yet, it is hard to avoid worrying when a job is lost, a home is in foreclosure, or a child is sick and there is no money for medicine. For all of us to be free to seek the Kingdom of God, we need a commitment from the entire human community to ensure everyone has enough: food, clothes, a place to live, work, and time to rest. How better than to start with the needs within our own community? Songs that focus on the dignity of all might help to inspire such a generosity.

Prayers
others may be added

To our loving and provident God, let us pray, saying:

▪ **Lord, hear us.**

That the Church may trust in God's guidance, we pray: ▪ That the poor may receive what they need from the earth's abundance, we pray: ▪ That we recognize the needs within our own community of music ministers and serve one another, we pray: ▪ That we may dedicate this day to the Lord who provides for us, we pray: ▪

Our Father . . .

Lord God,
you are the source of all that we have and all that we are.
Help us to trust in your abiding presence and your constant love for us.
Through Christ our Lord.
Amen.

Psalm
62:2–3, 6–7, 8–9 (6a)

R. Rest in God alone, my soul. R/.

† *In the name of the Father, and of the Son, and of the Holy Spirit. Amen.*

Again we keep this solemn fast,
A gift of faith from ages past,
This Lent which binds us lovingly
To faith and hope and charity.

—"Again We Keep This Solemn Fast"
(ERHALT UNS HERR)

The forty days of Lent are not literally forty, but the number evokes the use of all other uses of "forty" in the Scriptures. For forty days, Jesus fasted and prepared to proclaim the Good News. Long before Jesus, Moses and Elijah had their forty-day fasts. It rained on the earth and on Noah's ark for forty days, and the earth had a new beginning. And for forty years the people of Israel wandered in the wilderness toward the Promised Land. In the Bible, the number forty means that something important is taking place. We enter Lent with ashes on our heads, and we fast in various ways, perhaps by eating less food and foregoing treats. We give alms, which means that we find ways to share what we have: our time and our goods. In these ways, we remember our Baptism and try to grow more deeply in the Christian life.

† *In the name of the Father, and of the Son, and of the Holy Spirit. Amen.*

Psalm   51:3–4, 5–6ab, 12–13, 14 and 17
(see 3a)

R. Be merciful, O Lord, for we have sinned. R/.

Gospel   Matthew 6:1–4

Jesus said to his disciples: "Take care not to perform righteous deeds in order that people may see them; otherwise, you will have no recompense from your heavenly Father. When you give alms, do not blow a trumpet before you, as the hypocrites do in the synagogues and in the streets to win the praise of others. Amen, I say to you, they have received their reward. But when you give alms, do not let your left hand know what your right is doing, so that your almsgiving may be secret. And your Father who sees in secret will repay you."

Silent Reflection

Jesus says to do righteous deeds and give alms in secret and yet also says "your light must shine before others" (from a recent Gospel reading in Ordinary Time). A curious contradiction? Or as music ministers, can we *both* let the light of our talents shine *and* at the same time guard against seeking adulation? Can we hold the paradox of being in a ministry that invites praise, and yet have no personal desire for it? Let us take this day to reflect on why we do what we do as music ministers so as to be certain that our service is humble and genuine.

Prayers   others may be added

At the beginning of this joyful season, we pray:

▪ Lord, hear us.

For the renewal of the Church and all her members, we pray: ▪ For peace in the world, we pray: ▪ For those preparing for Baptism, we pray: ▪ For music directors, choir members, cantors, instrumentalists, and all artists, we pray: ▪ For all who keep this season of Lent, we pray: ▪

Our Father . . .

Lord God,
as we begin the holy discipline of
    Lent, may our prayer, fasting,
    and almsgiving make us more
    aware of your Spirit, dwelling
    in the secret of our hearts.
Through Christ our Lord.
Amen.

Psalm   51:3–4, 5–6ab, 12–13, 14 and 17
(see 3a)

R. Be merciful, O Lord, for we have sinned. R/.

† *In the name of the Father, and of the Son, and of the Holy Spirit. Amen.*

March 9, 2014

First Sunday of Lent

† *In the name of the Father, and of the Son, and of the Holy Spirit. Amen.*

Psalm 51:3–4, 5–6, 12–13, 17 (see 3a)

R. Be merciful, O Lord, for we have sinned. R/.

Gospel Matthew 4:1–4

At the time Jesus was led by the Spirit into the desert to be tempted by the devil. He fasted for forty days and forty nights, and afterwards he was hungry. The tempter approached and said to him, "If you are the Son of God, command that these stones become loaves of bread." He said in reply, "It is written: / *One does not live by bread alone, / but by every word that comes forth / from the mouth of God.*"

Silent Reflection

"One does not live by bread alone, but by every word that comes forth from the mouth of God." Since so many of the texts we sing are taken from Scripture, and since we believe our Scripture to be the Word of God, how blessed are we to be so nourished week in and week out! It's true that we take in this life-giving "food" of words through melodies and harmonies that allow the words to vibrate within every fiber of our being. Still, let us resist the temptation to move too quickly to the music lest we miss the beauty of the texts for their own sake.

Prayers *others may be added*

In this season of grace, we pray with confidence to God who can do all things:

▪ Lord, hear us.

Lord, grant unity and peace to your Church, we pray: ▪ Bring healing to the nations, we pray: ▪ Strengthen those among us preparing for Baptism, we pray: ▪ Be with those who are experiencing doubt and temptation, we pray: ▪ Inspire the composers and text writers who grace us with the fruits of their labor, we pray: ▪

Our Father . . .

Lord God,
be our strength in times of temptation:
   when we put our desires before
   the needs of others, when we twist
   Scripture to justify our actions,
   when we are hungry for power or
   for control: have mercy on us and
   strengthen us.
Through Christ our Lord.
Amen.

Psalm 51:3–4, 5–6, 12–13, 17 (see 3a)

R. Be merciful, O Lord, for we have sinned. R/.

† *In the name of the Father, and of the Son, and of the Holy Spirit. Amen.*

† In the name of the Father, and of the Son, and of the Holy Spirit. Amen.

Psalm
33:4–5, 18–19, 20, 22 (22)

R. Lord, let your mercy be on us, as we place our trust in you. R/.

Gospel
Matthew 17:1–5

Jesus took Peter, James, and John his brother, and led them up a high mountain by themselves. And he was transfigured before them; his face shone like the sun and his clothes became white as light. And behold, Moses and Elijah appeared to them, conversing with him. Then Peter said to Jesus in reply, "Lord, it is good that we are here. If you wish, I will make three tents here, one for you, one for Moses, and one for Elijah." While he was still speaking, behold, a bright cloud cast a shadow over them, then from the cloud came a voice that said, "This is my beloved Son, with whom I am well pleased; listen to him."

Silent Reflection

We count on one another to be faithful to our music ministry commitment. We count on the assembly to participate in their ministry as well. Sometimes it is so easy, like when we find ourselves in "mountaintop" moments of life. Other life circumstances can close us down and quiet our voices. Even the same event can bring joy to some and pain to others. Being in communion with one another surely means that someone will be there to sing the song for those who cannot until they lift up their voices once more.

Prayers
others may be added

Let us pray for the grace to respond to the Word of God, saying:

- Lord, hear us.

Fill the Church with your light, we pray: ▪ Inspire us to sing with passion for those who are without their song, we pray: ▪ Enlighten the minds and hearts of those preparing for Baptism, we pray: ▪ Help us to accept the suffering that comes to us as a gift from you, we pray: ▪

Our Father . . .

Lord Jesus Christ,
transfigured in glory, teach us to
    recognize your presence not only
    in the mountaintop moments of
    our lives, but in all of our sorrows.
You live and reign for ever and ever.
Amen.

Psalm
33:4–5, 18–19, 20, 22 (22)

R. Lord, let your mercy be on us, as we place our trust in you. R/.

† In the name of the Father, and of the Son, and of the Holy Spirit. Amen.

† *In the name of the Father, and of the Son, and of the Holy Spirit. Amen.*

Psalm   95:1–2, 6–7, 8–9 (8)

R. If today you hear his voice, harden not your hearts. R/.

Gospel   John 4:6–10

Jesus, tired from his journey, sat down there at the well. It was about noon.

A woman of Samaria came to draw water. Jesus said to her, "Give me a drink." His disciples had gone into the town to buy food. The Samaritan woman said to him, "How can you, a Jew, ask me, a Samaritan woman, for a drink?" . . . Jesus answered and said to her, "If you knew the gift of God and who is saying to you, 'Give me a drink,' you would have asked him and he would have given you living water."

Silent Reflection

Take a moment to remember how you were invited into the choir or music ministry. Was it a personal invitation or a bulletin request for new members? Was your response immediate? Did you take time to discern if this was a commitment you could make? As you pause to recall, take a few more minutes to give thanks for "how it all began," feeling gratitude for any people or any set of circumstances responsible for the invitation. Given that this has been something good in your life, might you invite another to be so gifted?

Prayers   *others may be added*

Let us ask the Lord to form a new heart within us as we pray:

- Give us living water.

Make your Church a source of living water for all people, we pray: ▪ Satisfy those who thirst for justice and peace, we pray: ▪ Strengthen the elect, preparing for Baptism, we pray: ▪ Help us to long for the living water that flows from your holy Word, we pray: ▪

Our Father . . .

Lord our God,
courage for the fearful, forgiveness for the sinful, comfort for the sorrowful, lead all people to drink of the living water that springs up for eternal life.
Through Christ our Lord.
Amen.

Psalm   95:1–2, 6–7, 8–9 (8)

R. If today you hear his voice, harden not your hearts. R/.

† *In the name of the Father, and of the Son, and of the Holy Spirit. Amen.*

† In the name of the Father, and of the Son, and of the Holy Spirit. Amen.

Psalm
23:1–3a, 3b–4, 5, 6 (1)

R. The Lord is my shepherd; there is nothing I shall want. R/.

Gospel
John 9:1–3, 5–7

As Jesus passed by he saw a man blind from birth. His disciples asked him, "Rabbi, who sinned, this man or his parents, that he was born blind?" Jesus answered, "Neither he nor his parents sinned; it is so that the works of God might be made visible through him." When he had said this, he spat on the ground and made clay with the saliva, and smeared the clay on his eyes, and said to him, "Go wash in the Pool of Siloam"—which means Sent—. So he went and washed, and came back able to see.

Silent Reflection

The choir community is a human community. Like in any other community, its members can fall prey to pettiness, narrow-mindedness, gossip, and judgment. Are we able to risk with one another enough to challenge those things inconsistent with Jesus's message of love? Where someone is blind to their negative actions, can we shine the light of awareness? Are we open to someone confronting our behavior when it is hurtful? If the need arose, would we trust one another to be honest with each other, and to forgive each other? It is something to think about.

Prayers
others may be added

Rejoicing in Christ, the light of the world, we pray:

▪ **Lord, give us light.**

Guide your Church, and make it a light to the whole world, we pray: ▪ Lead the nations in the ways of justice and peace, we pray: ▪ Bless those preparing for Baptism; lead them to the light of Christ, we pray: ▪ Strengthen in our music ministry community the desire to deepen as a community of love, we pray: ▪

Our Father . . .

Lord Jesus Christ,
you gave to the man born blind sight and insight, a future full of hope.
Help us to know our blindness and grant us healing and forgiveness, so that we may proclaim you as Messiah and Lord, who lives and reigns for ever and ever.
Amen.

Psalm
23:1–3a, 3b–4, 5, 6 (1)

R. The Lord is my shepherd; there is nothing I shall want. R/.

† In the name of the Father, and of the Son, and of the Holy Spirit. Amen.

† In the name of the Father, and of the Son, and of the Holy Spirit. Amen.

Psalm   130:1–2, 3–4, 5–6, 7–8 (7)

R. With the Lord there is mercy and fullness of redemption. R/.

Gospel   John 11:17–18, 19–27

When Jesus arrived, he found that Lazarus had already been in the tomb for four days. Now Bethany was near Jerusalem, only about two miles away. And many of the Jews had come to Martha and Mary to comfort them about their brother. When Martha heard that Jesus was coming, she went to meet him; but Mary sat at home. Martha said to Jesus, "Lord, if you had been here, my brother would not have died. But even now I know that whatever you ask of God, God will give you." Jesus said to her, "Your brother will rise."

Silent Reflection

Whether part of the funeral choir, a cantor, or a member of the parish choir in the assembly at a funeral liturgy, yours is a voice that is practiced in singing words of faith. Yours is a voice that can bring comfort in its unwavering strength and in its conviction regarding the sung texts that are chosen to help face loss with hope and promise. The assembly of mourners can lean on you. Sing out, that through your voice God can say to them, "Your loved one will rise!"

Prayers   *others may be added*

To Jesus Christ, who is the resurrection and the life, we pray:

- Give us new life.

Bless your Church; bring us to new life in you, we pray: ▪ Bring back those who have strayed and strengthen those whose faith is weak, we pray: ▪ Be with those preparing for the new life of Baptism, we pray: ▪ Help us to use our voices well in bringing comfort to those who mourn, we pray: ▪ Lead all our beloved dead into the light of your presence, we pray: ▪

Our Father . . .

Lord Jesus Christ,
when we feel dead in our sins, when we
        are burdened with grief, when we are
        lost in our doubts, call us forth with
        your word of power, set us free and
        give us life in your presence.
You live and reign for ever and ever.
Amen.

Psalm   130:1–2, 3–4, 5–6, 7–8 (7)

R. With the Lord there is mercy and fullness of redemption. R/.

† In the name of the Father, and of the Son, and of the Holy Spirit. Amen.

April 13, 2014

Palm Sunday of the Passion of the Lord

† *In the name of the Father, and of the Son, and of the Holy Spirit. Amen.*

Psalm   22:8–9, 17–18, 19–20, 23–24 (2a)
R. My God, my God, why have you abandoned me? R/.

Gospel   Matthew 26:20–25

When it was evening, [Jesus] reclined at table with the Twelve. And while they were eating, he said, "Amen, I say to you, one of you will betray me." Deeply distressed at this, they began to say to him one after another, "Surely it is not I, Lord?" He said in reply, "He who had dipped his hand into the dish with me is the one who will betray me. The Son of Man indeed goes, as it is written of him, but woe to that man by whom the Son of Man is betrayed. It would be better for that man if he had never been born." Then Judas, his betrayer, said in reply, "Surely it is not I, Rabbi?" He answered, "You have said so."

Silent Reflection

It takes strength of character to admit a wrongdoing. What if Judas had acknowledged what he was planning and asked for forgiveness instead of denying it? We all have "what ifs" from our lives, things that we regret, choices for which we may have expressed sorrow but that still hold us bound. As we enter this holiest of weeks with all its demands on the parish musicians, can we let go of any lingering sadness over transgressions of the past and be free to live in the fullness of these days? As a final preparation for Easter, can we ask for and trust in God's forgiveness?

Prayers   *others may be added*

We have set out with Jesus Christ, our King, on his journey to Jerusalem. In love, we pray:

▪ **Lord, have mercy on us.**

Renew the Church in the coming holy days, we pray: ▪ Bring peace to the nations and inner peace to every human person, we pray: ▪ Bless those preparing for Baptism; give them grace and strength, we pray: ▪ Open our hearts to grace and open our throats to sing in the fullness of those who know they are beloved of God, we pray: ▪ Fill all who celebrate Holy Week with reverence, awareness, wonder, and devotion, we pray: ▪

Our Father . . .

Lord Jesus Christ,
we have begun to follow you on the
*   journey that will lead us to the heart*
*   of your saving mysteries.*
During these holy days, may we come to
*   know you better than ever before, as*
*   our brother and friend, our teacher*
*   and master, our Lord and Savior.*
You live and reign for ever and ever.
Amen.

Psalm   22:8–9, 17–18, 19–20, 23–24 (2a)
R. My God, my God, why have you abandoned me? R/.

† *In the name of the Father, and of the Son, and of the Holy Spirit. Amen.*

The Sacred
Paschal Triduum

This is the night
that even now, throughout the world,
sets Christian believers apart from worldly vices
and from the gloom of sin,
leading them to grace
and joining them to his holy ones.

—The Easter Proclamation *(Exsultet)*,
The Roman Missal

Triduum means the "Three Days." For the Jewish people, Passover celebrates the great event when God delivered the people of Israel from slavery. The followers of Jesus proclaim that in the life, Passion, Death, and Resurrection of Jesus, God has freed and saved us. When Lent ends, we stand at the heart of the liturgical year. On the night of Holy Saturday, we keep the Easter Vigil. We gather to light a great fire and a towering candle, to listen to our most treasured Scriptures, and to sing psalms and other songs. Then we gather around the waters of the font as those who have been preparing for new life in Christ receive the Sacraments of Initiation. The newly baptized are then anointed with a fragrant oil called *chrism*; and, at last, with these newly baptized, who are now called *neophytes*, we celebrate the Eucharist.

We prepare for this Vigil by celebrating the institution of the Holy Eucharist on Holy Thursday and by commemorating the Lord's Passion by adoring the Cross on Good Friday. We also prepare by keeping the Paschal fast, a special fast of Good Friday and Holy Saturday. The Church fasts—from food, from entertainment, from chatter, from work—so we have time to ponder deeply the Death and Resurrection of the Lord, the mystery of faith that we will celebrate in our Vigil.

† *In the name of the Father, and of the Son, and of the Holy Spirit. Amen.*

Psalm
116:12–13, 15–16bc, 17–18
(see 1 Corinthians 10:16)

R. Our blessing-cup is a communion with the Blood of Christ. R/.

Gospel
John 13:6–9, 12–14

He [Jesus] came to Simon Peter, who said to him, "Master, are you going to wash my feet?" Jesus answered and said to him, "What I am doing you do not understand now, but you will understand later." Peter said to him, "You will never wash my feet." Jesus answered him," Unless I wash you, you will have no inheritance with me." Simon Peter said to him, "Master, then not only my feet but my hands and head as well."

"Do you realize what I have done for you? You call me 'teacher' and 'master,' and rightly so, for indeed I am. If I, therefore, the master and teacher have washed your feet, you ought to wash one another's feet."

Silent Reflection

Music and singing most often accompany the washing of feet during the Holy Thursday liturgy. Focused on providing the music, we likely cannot be present to the ritual in the same way as most of the assembly. Perhaps we don't see the faces of those washing and being washed. Yet, as we rehearse for the ritual, we have a chance to think about the vulnerability and the surrender that foot washing invites. What does such a reflection tell you about your understanding of service? Where is there room for growth?

Prayers
others may be added

We call upon Christ, priest and servant, as we pray:

▪ **Lord, have mercy on us.**

For the Church, nourished and made one by the Body and Blood of Christ, we pray: ▪ For bishops and priests, ministers of a special calling, we pray: ▪ For those in our parish music ministry who seek a deeper understanding of how we are all servants to one another, we pray: ▪ For the grace to enter into the Three Days with heart and mind, we pray: ▪

Our Father . . .

Lord Jesus Christ,
you are in our midst as one who serves.
May all who have become members of
your Body by Baptism follow your
example of self-giving service so
that the world may come to believe.
You live and reign for ever and ever.
Amen.

Psalm
116:12–13, 15–16bc, 17–18
(see 1 Corinthians 10:16)

R. Our blessing-cup is a communion with the Blood of Christ. R/.

† *In the name of the Father, and of the Son, and of the Holy Spirit. Amen.*

April 18, 2014
Friday of the Passion of the Lord (Good Friday)

† *In the name of the Father, and of the Son, and of the Holy Spirit. Amen.*

Psalm
31:2, 6, 12–13, 15–16, 17, 25
(Luke 23:46)

R. Father, into your hands I commend my spirit. R/.

Gospel
John 19:25–27

Standing by the cross of Jesus were his mother and his mother's sister, Mary the wife of Clopas, and Mary of Magdala. When Jesus saw his mother and the disciple there whom he loved he said to his mother, "Woman, behold, your son." Then he said to the disciple, "Behold, your mother." And from that hour the disciple took her into his home.

Silent Reflection

Even in his last painful moments, Jesus was taking care of those he held most dear, making sure both his mother and "the disciple whom he loved" knew they were not left alone, but rather were given to one another in a new relationship of kinship: mother and son. In the most unlikely moment, Jesus was still revealing expectations around care-taking, being a safe haven to those in need, and being family to one another. How are your community, your parish, your family, and your choir welcoming places? How are you brother, sister, mother, father, son, and daughter to all?

Prayers
others may be added

To our crucified Lord, we pray:

▪ Lord, have mercy on us.

For the holy Church of God, for our Holy Father, for the bishops, priests, deacons, religious, and lay faithful, we pray: ▪ For those preparing for Baptism, that the Sign of the Cross may lead them to new life, we pray: ▪ For the sick, the dying, those unjustly deprived of liberty, and those suffering the ravages of war, we pray: ▪ For those new to our music ministry this year, that our deepening friendships will bring a sense of "being home" within our faith community, we pray: ▪

Our Father . . .

Lord Jesus Christ,
living and true, teach us the secret of your
      Cross: the hope of the hopeless,
      the comfort of the afflicted, the
      Tree of Life, the joy of the Church.
You live and reign for ever and ever.
Amen.

Psalm
31:2, 6, 12–13, 15–16, 17, 25
(Luke 23:46)

R. Father, into your hands I commend my spirit. R/.

† *In the name of the Father, and of the Son, and of the Holy Spirit. Amen.*

† *In the name of the Father, and of the Son, and of the Holy Spirit. Amen.*

Exodus   *15:1–2, 3–4, 5–6, 17–18 (1b)*

R. Let us sing to the Lord; he has covered himself in glory. R/.

Gospel   *Matthew 28:8–10*

[Mary Magdalene and the other Mary] went away quickly from the tomb, fearful yet overjoyed, and ran to announce [the news] to his disciples. And behold, Jesus met them on their way and greeted them. They approached, embraced his feet, and did him homage. Then Jesus said to them, "Do not be afraid. Go tell my brothers to go to Galilee, and there they will see me."

Silent Reflection

How glorious to be a part of the music ministry leading the "Alleluia" this night after so many weeks of not hearing it! There is such joy in the sound. In the Gospel, the women have joy at seeing the empty tomb, yet it is mixed with fear. Jesus knows this and meets them on their way, greeting them with the words, "Do not be afraid." This is a message to us as well. Live a faith that holds the power of the Resurrection as stronger than our fears. Live each moment in trust of a God who loves us unconditionally and is with us in all.

Prayers   *others may be added*

To the Lord of life, let us pray, saying:

▪ **Give us new life.**

For the Church, that we may be renewed by the celebration of the Resurrection of the Lord, we pray: ▪ For all those who will be baptized this night, we pray: ▪ For all who suffer from depression and for all who feel their lives lack meaning, that the Resurrection of Jesus Christ from the dead may fill them with light and hope, we pray: ▪ For all who raise their voice to sing "Alleluia" this night, that their lives will echo this sound of freedom and joy, we pray: ▪ For all who have died in the peace of God, that they may share in the power of Christ's victory over death, we pray: ▪

Our Father . . .

Christ, Son of the living God,
may the power of your Resurrection from
*   the dead transform the world.*
May it bring joy to all believers, comfort
*   to all who mourn, and hope to all*
*   who do not yet believe.*
You live and reign for ever and ever.
Amen.

Exodus   *15:1–2, 3–4, 5–6, 17–18 (1b)*

R. Let us sing to the Lord; he has covered himself in glory. R/.

† *In the name of the Father, and of the Son, and of the Holy Spirit. Amen.*

Easter Time

. . . overcome with paschal joy,
every land, every people exults in your praise
and even the heavenly Powers, with the
*   angelic hosts*
sing together the unending hymn of your glory,
as they acclaim:
Holy, Holy, Holy Lord God of hosts . . .

—Preface, Pentecost Sunday,
The Roman Missal

Easter Time lasts for fifty days. Easter Sunday is to the year what Sunday is to the week. We live as if God's Kingdom has already come—because it has. We put aside our fasting for feasting and celebration. We bless ourselves with baptismal water to remind us of our share in Jesus's Passion, Death, and Resurrection. "Alleluia" is our song because we delight to praise the Lord. The stories we read from Scripture are of Thomas's and Mary Magdalene's encounters with the Risen Lord, of meals with Jesus, of the Good Shepherd, and of the outpouring of the Holy Spirit.

April 20, 2014

Easter Sunday of the Resurrection of the Lord

† *In the name of the Father, and of the Son, and of the Holy Spirit. Amen.*

Psalm
118:1–2, 16–17, 22–23 (24)

R. This is the day the Lord has made; let us rejoice and be glad. R/.

OR: R. Alleluia. R/.

Gospel
John 20:1–8

On the first day of the week, Mary of Magdala came to the tomb early in the morning, while it was still dark, and saw the stone removed from the tomb. So she ran and went to Simon Peter and to the other disciple whom Jesus loved, and told them, "They have taken the Lord from the tomb, and we don't know where they put him." So Peter and the other disciple went out and came to the tomb. They both ran, but the other disciple ran faster than Peter and arrived at the tomb first; he bent down and saw the burial cloths there, but did not go in. When Simon Peter arrived after him, he went into the tomb and saw the burial cloths there, and the cloth that had covered his head, not with the burial cloths but rolled up in a separate place. Then the other disciple also went in, the one who had arrived at the tomb first, and he saw and believed.

Silent Reflection

What is a memory you have of being overcome so completely that all you could do was run and tell someone about your experience? Take a moment to relive that time and feel the emotion that rose up within you. Imagine what emotions must fill the hearts of the newly baptized. As they enter into a time of *mystagogia* during the fifty days of Easter Time, can we who have journeyed with them in their preparation time also open ourselves to be deepened in the faith we profess?

Prayers
others may be added

To the Lord who burst the bonds of death, we pray:

- **Risen Lord, hear our prayer.**

That the whole Church may be renewed by the celebration of this feast, we pray: ▪ That the hope of Christ's Resurrection may touch the hearts of those who live in the shadow of death and war, we pray: ▪ That as faith-filled musicians we will risk entering the "tomb" of our deeper selves to discover anew what it is we believe, we pray: ▪

Our Father . . .

Lord Jesus Christ,
we praise and glorify you on this day of
*   your victory.*
May the glorious fact of your Resurrection
*   dispel our doubts and fears, so that*
*   we may serve your people on earth*
*   until we rejoice with you in heaven.*
You live and reign for ever and ever.
Amen.

Psalm
118:1–2, 16–17, 22–23 (24)

R. This is the day the Lord has made; let us rejoice and be glad.   R/.

OR: R. Alleluia. R/.

† *In the name of the Father, and of the Son, and of the Holy Spirit. Amen.*

✝ In the name of the Father, and of the Son, and of the Holy Spirit. Amen.

Psalm   118:2–4, 13–15, 22–24 (11)

R. Give thanks to the Lord, for he is good, his love is everlasting. R/.

OR: R. Alleluia. R/.

Gospel   John 20:24–29

Thomas, called Didymus, one of the Twelve, was not with them when Jesus came. So the other disciples said to him, "We have seen the Lord." But Thomas said to them, "Unless I see the mark of the nails in his hands and put my finger into the nailmarks and put my hand into his side, I will not believe."

Now a week later his disciples were again inside and Thomas was with them. Jesus came, although the doors were locked, and stood in their midst and said, "Peace be with you." Then he said to Thomas, "Put your finger here and see my hands, and bring your hand and put it into my side, and do not be unbelieving, but believe." Thomas answered and said to him, "My Lord and my God!" Jesus said to him, "Have you come to believe because you have seen me? Blessed are those who have not seen and have believed."

Silent Reflection

Doesn't everything belong? Can we be fully human without the willingness to embrace everything in ourselves, even the shadow of our doubts and fears and those things we would rather not face or know about—things we have pushed aside or ignored? Jesus mercifully honors the doubt in Thomas and yet challenges him as well. There is more to knowing than what we can see, hear, and touch on the physical plane. As people of the Resurrection, we need not be afraid to trust what we know with our hearts and within our spirits.

Prayers   others may be added

To the crucified and risen One, we pray:

▪ **In your divine mercy, hear us, O Lord.**

That the Church may be a sign and an instrument of the divine mercy of God, we pray: ▪ That those who doubt God's love for them may put their trust in his divine mercy, we pray: ▪ That the newly baptized may find in the Eucharist the food for the journey to eternal life, we pray: ▪ That our community of musicians will be a safe place for sharing all of who we are, what we need, and what we believe, we pray: ▪

Our Father . . .

Risen Lord,
in this season of surpassing grace, renew the living spring of your life within us, and let us share the joy of all the newly baptized.
You live and reign for ever and ever. Amen.

Psalm   118:2–4, 13–15, 22–24 (11)

R. Give thanks to the Lord, for he is good, his love is everlasting. R/.

OR: R. Alleluia. R/.

✝ In the name of the Father, and of the Son, and of the Holy Spirit. Amen.

† *In the name of the Father, and of the Son, and of the Holy Spirit. Amen.*

Psalm　　　　16:1–2, 5, 7–8, 9–10, 11 (11a)

R. Lord, you will show us the path of life. R/.

OR: R. Alleluia. R/.

Gospel　　　　Luke 24:28–32

As [the disciples] approached the village to which they were going, [Jesus] gave the impression that he was going on farther. But they urged him, "Stay with us, for it is nearly evening and the day is almost over." So he went in to stay with them. And it happened that, while he was with them at table, he took bread, said the blessing, broke it, and gave it to them. With that their eyes were opened and they recognized him, but he vanished from their sight. Then they said to each other, "Were not our hearts burning within us while he spoke to us on the way and opened the Scriptures to us?"

Silent Reflection

There can be a hole in the fabric of our choir when someone leaves or is absent, be it a member or the director. Or, sometimes there is relief; for whatever reason, that person wasn't a good fit. Who are you in relationship to the whole? Do you embody the spirit of Jesus in how you share yourself with others? Let someone know when they are missed or when you're happy to see them. For you, it means noticing a "heart burning within" in their presence. For them, it is an affirmation that might be just what they need in that moment. For both, it is a blessing.

Prayers　　　　*others may be added*

To the Lord who comes to us in word and bread, we pray:

▪ **Christ, hear us.**

That the Church may recognize the presence of Christ, who opens the Scriptures for us and breaks the bread, we pray: ▪ That children, catechumens, and all who are learning the faith may come to love the Scriptures as they seek Christ in his Word, we pray: ▪ That all the hungry of the world may have enough to eat, we pray: ▪ That as ministers we be attuned to building up the Body of Christ in our words, gestures, and actions, we pray: ▪

Our Father . . .

Stay with us, Lord Jesus, and be our companion on life's way.
Like the disciples of old, may we listen to you as you open the Scriptures for us and come to know you as never before in the breaking of the bread.
You are Lord for ever and ever.
Amen.

Psalm　　　　16:1–2, 5, 7–8, 9–10, 11 (11a)

R. Lord, you will show us the path of life. R/.

OR: R. Alleluia. R/.

† *In the name of the Father, and of the Son, and of the Holy Spirit. Amen.*

May 11, 2014

Fourth Sunday of Easter

† *In the name of the Father, and of the Son, and of the Holy Spirit. Amen.*

Psalm
23:1–3a, 3b–4, 5, 6 (1)

R. The Lord is my shepherd; there is nothing I shall want. R/.

OR: R. Alleluia. R/.

Gospel
John 10:7–10

Jesus said again, "Amen, amen, I say to you, I am the gate for the sheep. All who came before me are thieves and robbers, but the sheep did not listen to them. I am the gate. Whoever enters through me will be saved, and will come in and go out and find pasture. A thief comes only to steal and slaughter and destroy; I came so that they might have life and have it more abundantly."

Silent Reflection

In Jesus's time, being a shepherd was a lowly station. Yet, Jesus uses the image of a shepherd in such a positive and vital way. Today, many whose work we cannot do without are the least paid and the least recognized. We still live in a "comparison/competition" world. One gift of being in the choir is that your job in the world outside of rehearsal doesn't matter. All are equal in the love of music-making. There is a lesson here, perhaps. Instead of asking "What do you do?" ask "What makes you happy?" Might this be a gateway to a more meaningful relationship with another?

Prayers
others may be added

To Christ, who guides and cares for his people, we pray:

▪ Shepherd of the sheep, hear us.

That the bishops and priests of the Church may model their ministry on that of the Good Shepherd, we pray: ▪ That all in authority over others may put the needs of the flock ahead of their own needs, we pray: ▪ That those who have gone astray may respond to the loving call of the Savior, we pray: ▪ That in a spirit of living life more abundantly, we may be intentional in both eliminating the illusion of separateness and fostering the reality of our connectedness, we pray: ▪ That we may be simple and humble of heart, following Christ our Shepherd wherever he may lead us, we pray: ▪

Our Father . . .

*Lord Jesus Christ,
Good Shepherd, you have called us by name, and we are yours.
May we express our faith in you by our love and care for your flock.
You live and reign for ever and ever.
Amen.*

Psalm
23:1–3a, 3b–4, 5, 6 (1)

R. The Lord is my shepherd; there is nothing I shall want. R/.

OR: R. Alleluia. R/.

† *In the name of the Father, and of the Son, and of the Holy Spirit. Amen.*

May 18, 2014
Fifth Sunday of Easter

† In the name of the Father, and of the Son, and of the Holy Spirit. Amen.

Psalm
33:1–2, 4–5, 18–19 (22)

R. Lord, let your mercy be on us, as we place our trust in you. R/.

OR: R. Alleluia. R/.

Gospel
John 14:1–6

Jesus said to his disciples, "Do not let your hearts be troubled. You have faith in God; have faith also in me. In my Father's house there are many dwelling places. If there were not, would I have told you that I am going to prepare a place for you? And if I go and prepare a place for you, I will come back again and take you to myself, so that where I am you also may be. Where I am going you know the way." Thomas said to him, "Master, we do not know where you are going; how can we know the way?" Jesus said to him, "I am the way and the truth and the life. No one comes to the Father except through me."

Silent Reflection

Instead of using the word *Christian*, we could say we are "people of the Way"—the way of Jesus the Christ. From our Baptism until death, we unpack what this means for us individually and in relationship with others. It is comforting to hear Jesus's words regarding a place prepared for us. We trust that following "the way" will lead to the fullness of eternity with Jesus as promised. There is no need to be troubled. Then, let our focus be on following the way of Jesus for the life of the world here and now. St. Catherine of Sienna said, "All the way to heaven *is* heaven."

Prayers
others may be added

To Christ, who is our Way, our Truth, and our Life, we pray:

▪ Lord, hear our prayer.

That all Christians may stay close to Christ, who is the Way, we pray: ▪ That those who struggle with doubt and those who have lost their faith may come to Christ, who is the Truth, we pray: ▪ That those who have died may come into the presence of Christ, who is the Life, we pray: ▪ That in Christ we no longer worry for the future or hold concern over the past and sing out our song in the freedom of this present, we pray: ▪

Our Father . . .

Lord Jesus Christ,
you are Light of the World, Shepherd and
Vine, Bread and Cup, Way, Truth,
and Life.
May we abide in you always, who are Lord
for ever and ever.
Amen.

Psalm
33:1–2, 4–5, 18–19 (22)

R. Lord, let your mercy be on us, as we place our trust in you. R/.

OR: R. Alleluia. R/.

† In the name of the Father, and of the Son, and of the Holy Spirit. Amen.

Sixth Sunday of Easter

† *In the name of the Father, and of the Son, and of the Holy Spirit. Amen.*

Psalm
66:1–3, 4–5, 6–7, 16, 20 (1)

R. Let all the earth cry out to God with joy. R/.

OR: R. Alleluia. R/.

Gospel
John 14:15–17

Jesus said to his disciples: "If you love me, you will keep my commandments. And I will ask the Father, and he will give you another Advocate to be with you always, the Spirit of truth, whom the world cannot accept, because it neither sees nor knows him. But you know him, because he remains with you, and will be in you."

Silent Reflection

If you love me . . . Can we stop and linger over these words? Yes, Jesus follows them with "keep my commandments." These three words might also provide a fruitful reflection. For now, however, let us each simply take the first four words of the Scripture passage into our hearts and wait for them to speak to us in this moment of our life. *If you love me . . .* what? Dare we open ourselves to find out what the Spirit within, the Spirit of Truth, wants to reveal to us? To grow spiritually, to deepen in faith, we must.

Prayers
others may be added

To the Lord we love, we pray, saying:

▪ Christ, hear us.

That the Church may express her love for the Lord by her care for the poor, we pray: ▪ That the nations may lay down their weapons of hate and seek peace, we pray: ▪ That those who feel abandoned may know the presence of the comforter, the Holy Spirit, we pray: ▪ That we who cherish bringing beautiful sounds into the world can wait in silence for Divine Grace to reveal where Love beckons us, we pray: ▪

Our Father . . .

Lord Jesus Christ,
we love you.
May we show our love for you by keeping your commandment of love, and serving those whom you love.
You are Lord for ever and ever.
Amen.

Psalm
66:1–3, 4–5, 6–7, 16, 20 (1)

R. Let all the earth cry out to God with joy. R/.

OR: R. Alleluia. R/.

† *In the name of the Father, and of the Son, and of the Holy Spirit. Amen.*

May 29/June 1, 2014
Solemnity of the Ascension of the Lord

† *In the name of the Father, and of the Son, and of the Holy Spirit. Amen.*

Psalm
47:2–3, 6–7, 8–9 (6)

R. God mounts his throne to shouts of joy: a blare of trumpets for the Lord. R/.

OR: R. Alleluia. R/.

Gospel
Matthew 28:16–20

The eleven disciples went to Galilee, to the mountain to which Jesus had ordered them. When they saw him, they worshiped, but they doubted. Then Jesus approached and said to them, "All power in heaven and on earth has been given to me. Go, therefore, and make disciples of all nations, baptizing them in the name of the Father, and of the Son, and of the Holy Spirit, teaching them to observe all that I have commanded you. And behold, I am with you always, until the end of the age."

Silent Reflection

This is quite a mandate from Jesus to his disciples, to "go and make disciples of all nations." Is it not our mandate, too, to bring the Light of Christ to the world in the way we can? Yet we, like those early disciples, are not on our own. We know this not just because we read in Scripture that Jesus is with us "until the end of the age." We know this through our experiences of seeing the face of God in one another or of hearing God's voice in words of encouragement. Behind each act of reaching out in faith is the support of Christ present in our community of faith.

Prayers
others may be added

To Christ, ascended into heaven, we pray:

▪ **Lord, hear us.**

That the Church may reach out with compassion to the poor and the afflicted and raise them up, we pray: ▪ That all who believe in Christ may rejoice in him continually, giving praise to God, we pray: ▪ That those who long to experience God's presence may find him in his Holy Spirit, we pray: ▪ That we who minister together as singers and instrumentalists may continually pray for one another to have the courage to witness the faith we proclaim in our music and song, we pray: ▪

Our Father . . .

Risen and ascended Lord,
though you have ascended to your Father,
you are still with us; and though
we are on earth, we are already
with you.
May we who live between heaven and
earth reach out with your love to
those who are bowed down by
poverty, illness, or grief.
You are Lord for ever and ever.
Amen.

Psalm
47:2–3, 6–7, 8–9 (6)

R. God mounts his throne to shouts of joy: a blare of trumpets for the Lord. R/.

OR: R. Alleluia. R/.

† *In the name of the Father, and of the Son, and of the Holy Spirit. Amen.*

June 1, 2014
Seventh Sunday of Easter

† *In the name of the Father, and of the Son, and of the Holy Spirit. Amen.*

Psalm
27:1, 4, 7–8 (13)

R. I believe that I shall see the good things of the Lord in the land of the living. R/.

OR: R. Alleluia. R/.

Gospel
John 17:1–11a

Jesus raised his eyes to heaven and said, "Father, the hour has come. Give glory to your son, so that your son may glorify you, just as you gave him authority over all people, so that your son may give eternal life to all you gave him. Now this is eternal life, that they should know you, the only true God, and the one whom you sent, Jesus Christ. I glorified you on earth by accomplishing the work that you gave me to do. Now glorify me, Father, with you, with the glory that I had with you before the world began."

Silent Reflection

Oh, to know that you have accomplished the work you were given to do in this world! Can such a blessing be ours? As long as we continue to do the spiritual work of "waking up" to our true nature as God's beloved, as long as we keep opening our hearts to the oneness we share with all of creation, as long as our actions give glory to the Creator of all, as long as when we falter we get up again and start anew on a path of love, we are living the essence of why we are here. Our ministry in music is but a way given to us to help in the work of our lives here on earth.

Prayers
others may be added

To our risen and ascended Lord, we pray:

▪ **Lord, remain with us always.**

That all the baptized may be united in love and in prayer to the Father, we pray: ▪ That the gifts of the Holy Spirit may be poured out on all people, we pray: ▪ That Christ's own peace may dawn in our troubled world, we pray: ▪ That Christ may be glorified in us every day and that we may glorify God in the songs we sing each week, we pray: ▪

Our Father . . .

Lord God,
draw us into your divine love.
May we accept one another, reach out to one another, and love one another, until that day when we behold you face to face.
We ask this through Christ our Lord. Amen.

Psalm
27:1, 4, 7–8 (13)

R. I believe that I shall see the good things of the Lord in the land of the living. R/.

OR: R. Alleluia. R/.

† *In the name of the Father, and of the Son, and of the Holy Spirit. Amen.*

June 8, 2014

Solemnity of Pentecost

† *In the name of the Father, and of the Son, and of the Holy Spirit. Amen.*

Psalm 104:1, 24, 29–30, 31, 34 *(see 30)*

R. Lord, send out your Spirit, and renew the face of the earth. R/.

OR: R. Alleluia. R/.

Gospel John 20:19–23

On the evening of that first day of the week, when the doors were locked, where the disciples were, for fear of the Jews, Jesus came and stood in their midst and said to them, "Peace be with you." When he had said this, he showed them his hands and his side. The disciples rejoiced when they saw the Lord. Jesus said to them again, "Peace be with you. As the Father has sent me, so I send you." And when he had said this, he breathed on them and said to them, "Receive the Holy Spirit. Whose sins you forgive are forgiven them, and whose sins you retain are retained."

Silent Reflection

Peace be with you, a peace beyond understanding. A peace that can loosen the bonds of fear. An inner peace that opens us to forgive and to be forgiven, and so much more. Such a peace is within us, although perhaps hard to discover amid the demands and the rush of modern living. Has the journey through Lent and Easter Time stirred in you a desire for more ways to nurture your spirit besides your music ministry? Find a spiritual practice and enter into its discipline. A spiritual companion can be helpful as a guide as well. Listen well to what your heart is saying.

Prayers *others may be added*

For the gifts of the Holy Spirit, we pray:

▪ **Come, Holy Spirit!**

For the Spirit of wisdom and understanding, we pray: ▪ For the Spirit of courage and right judgment, we pray: ▪ For the Spirit of knowledge, we pray: ▪ For the Spirit of piety and reverence, we pray: ▪ For a contemplative Spirit to enrich the prayer of our song, we pray: ▪

Our Father . . .

Come, Holy Spirit,
as on the day of Pentecost.
Bend our stubborn hearts, melt our cold
*   hearts, cleanse our sinful hearts,*
*   so that we may give ourselves*
*   wholly to you and bring your love*
*   to a waiting world.*
We ask this through Christ our Lord.
Amen.

Psalm 104:1, 24, 29–30, 31, 34 *(see 30)*

R. Lord, send out your Spirit, and renew the face of the earth. R/.

OR: R. Alleluia. R/.

† *In the name of the Father, and of the Son, and of the Holy Spirit. Amen.*

Ordinary Time

During Summer and Fall

The Paschal hymn, of course,
does not cease when a liturgical
celebration ends. Christ, whose
praises we have sung, remains with
us and leads us through church doors
to the whole world, with its joys and
hopes, griefs and anxieties.[1]

—*Sing to the Lord: Music in Divine Worship,* 8

Ordinary comes from the word ordinal, and means "counted." We use this word for this period of time not because it is "boring" time, but because we count the days. We will remain in Ordinary Time for the rest of the liturgical year, until a new liturgical year begins with Advent in November. Ordinary Time is full of solemnities, feasts, and memorials of the Lord and the saints. With the saints and Scriptures as our guide, we use this time to grow in discipleship.

---

1.   See Second Vatican Council, *Gaudium et Spes (Pastoral Constitution on the Church in the Modern World)*, no. 1.

† In the name of the Father, and of the Son, and of the Holy Spirit. Amen.

Daniel
3:52, 53, 54, 55 (52b)

R. Glory and praise for ever! R/.

Gospel
John 3:16–18

God so loved the world that he gave his only Son, so that everyone who believes in him might not perish but might have eternal life. For God did not send his Son into the world to condemn the world, but that the world might be saved through him. Whoever believes in him will not be condemned, but whoever does not believe has already been condemned, because he has not believed in the name of the only Son of God.

Silent Reflection

Musical pieces have different degrees of difficulty. Some might be beyond the capacity of a particular choir, or written for voices a specific choir doesn't have. The limitations that keep a piece from our grasp at any point in time won't necessarily always be there. Though we will never fully understand the Love within the Trinity incarnated in Jesus, it is enough to know that we are held in the beauty of this Love poured out in abundance. We must not limit the depth of our loving in return. Rather, we should continue to grow in the capacity to love. Love is limitless.

Prayers
others may be added

To our God, the Blessed Trinity of love, let us pray:

- **Lord, hear our prayer.**

For the Church, that we may be a community of love, sharing each other's joys and sorrows, we pray: ▪ For families, that they may be united in peace by the love of the Blessed Trinity, we pray: ▪ For the world, that the divisions among us may be healed, we pray: ▪ For all who have died, that they may behold God face to face, we pray: ▪ For our choir members and musicians, that as we greatly desire to expand musically, we yearn even more greatly for fuller unity in relationships, we pray: ▪

Our Father . . .

We worship you, O God our Father.
With your Son our Savior and the Spirit
of our love, you are the one God.
May our faith in you transform our lives,
so that we may be instruments of
your love for all we meet.
We ask this through Christ our Lord.
Amen.

Daniel
3:52, 53, 54, 55 (52b)

R. Glory and praise for ever! R/.

† In the name of the Father, and of the Son, and of the Holy Spirit. Amen.

† In the name of the Father, and of the Son, and of the Holy Spirit. Amen.

Psalm
147:12–13, 14–15, 19–20 (12)

R. Praise the Lord, Jerusalem. R/.

OR: R. Alleluia. R/.

Gospel
John 6:52–58

The Jews quarreled among themselves, saying, "How can this man give us his flesh to eat?" Jesus said to them, "Amen, amen, I say to you, unless you eat the flesh of the Son of Man and drink his blood, you do not have life within you. Whoever eats my flesh and drinks my blood has eternal life, and I will raise him on the last day. For my flesh is true food, and my blood is true drink. Whoever eats my flesh and drinks my blood remains in me and I in him. Just as the living Father sent me and I have life because of the Father, so also the one who feeds on me will have life because of me. This is the bread that came down from heaven. Unlike your ancestors who ate and still died, whoever eats this bread will live forever."

Silent Reflection

"Amen" we say to the Bread and to the Wine offered in Communion at liturgy. It is our "yes" to becoming more like Jesus. As St. Augustine said, "Receive what you are; become what you receive." The choir is often, if not always, receiving Communion just before, just after, or even during the singing of the Communion song. Let this not keep us from being mindful of what we are doing in the ritual action of receiving the Body and Blood of Jesus. Even if just for a moment, take in the wonderment of all that your "Amen" implies.

Prayers
others may be added

To the Lord who feeds and sustains his people, we pray:

▪ **Christ Jesus, bread of heaven, hear our prayer.**

That the Church may be strengthened through the celebration of the Eucharist, we pray: ▪ That all who hunger may have an abundance of good things, we pray: ▪ That as ministers we learn to listen beyond the words we hear and to pay attention to what rises up within us as our heart's response, we pray: ▪ That we may be filled with wonder, reverence, and love every time we approach the table of the Lord, we pray: ▪

Our Father . . .

Christ Jesus, bread of heaven,
*   hear our prayer.*
Thou who all things canst and knowest,
Who on earth such food bestowest,
Grant us with thy saints, though lowest,
Where the heavenly feast thou showest,
Fellow heirs and guests to be.
You live and reign for ever and ever.
Amen.

(From Lauda Sion, *the Sequence for Corpus Christi*)

Psalm
147:12–13, 14–15, 19–20 (12)

R. Praise the Lord, Jerusalem. R/.

OR: R. Alleluia. R/.

† In the name of the Father, and of the Son, and of the Holy Spirit. Amen.

June 29, 2014
Solemnity of Sts. Peter and Paul, Apostles

† In the name of the Father, and of the Son, and of the Holy Spirit. Amen.

Psalm 34:2–3, 4–5, 6–7, 8–9 (5b)

R. The angel of the Lord will rescue those who fear him. R/.

Gospel John 21:15–19

[Jesus] said to Simon Peter, "Simon, son of John, do you love me more than these?" He said to him, "Yes, Lord, you know that I love you." He said to him, "Feed my lambs." He then said to him a second time, "Simon, son of John, do you love me?" He said to him, "Yes, Lord, you know that I love you." He said to him, "Tend my sheep." He said to him the third time, "Simon, son of John, do you love me?" Peter was distressed that he had said to him a third time, "Do you love me?" and he said to him, "Lord, you know everything; you know that I love you." Jesus said to him, "Feed my sheep."

Silent Reflection

How often do we hear, yet do not really listen? Sometimes this can lead to frustration, like when the music director has to repeat instructions multiple times because choir members aren't really listening. Sometimes, however, there is value in hearing something repeated. We take in not just with our heads, but with our hearts. When we speak or sing something over and over, like a mantra, it is hoped that we understand more of what the words mean for us. What do you respond to Jesus asking, "Do you love me?" Then, what is Jesus's response back to you? Listen.

Prayers others may be added

The Lord has built his Church on the rock foundation of the Apostles' faith. In faith we pray:

▪ **Bless your Church, Lord.**

That the Church may be steadfast in faith, hope, and love, we pray: ▪ That bishops, priests, deacons, and religious may be models of wisdom, love, and right living, we pray: ▪ That those who have never heard the message of Christ may have the Good News preached to them, we pray: ▪ That as music ministers we learn to listen beyond the words we hear in order to pay attention to what rises up within us as our hearts' response, we pray: ▪ That the example of Sts. Peter and Paul may fill us with new zeal for God's service, we pray: ▪

Our Father . . .

Lord,
you know everything; you know that
*   we love you.*
May we be mindful of our weaknesses,
*   like your holy Apostles Peter and*
*   Paul, and may we rise with new*
*   strength to love you more and more*
*   and to transform the world into the*
*   kingdom of your promise.*
You live and reign for ever and ever.
Amen.

Psalm 34:2–3, 4–5, 6–7, 8–9 (5b)

R. The angel of the Lord will rescue those who fear him. R/.

† In the name of the Father, and of the Son, and of the Holy Spirit. Amen.

† *In the name of the Father, and of the Son, and of the Holy Spirit. Amen.*

Psalm 145:1–2, 8–9, 10–11, 13–14 (see 1)
R. I will praise your name for ever, my king and my God. R/.
OR: R. Alleluia. R/.

Gospel Matthew 11:25–27

At that time Jesus exclaimed: "I give praise to you, Father, Lord of heaven and earth, for although you have hidden these things from the wise and the learned you have revealed them to little ones. Yes, Father, such has been your gracious will. All things have been handed over to me by my Father. No one knows the Son except the Father, and no one knows the Father except the Son and anyone to whom the Son wishes to reveal him."

Silent Reflection

One thing revealed to the childlike that the "wise" can forget at times is that we cannot go it alone. When we are burdened with any manner of sadness or concern, no shame, pride, or fear of judgment should stand in the way of reaching out to another, or of asking for help. Whom can you entrust with this part of yourself? Pray for guidance. Perhaps it is even the person you sit next to or near to in your section of the choir, someone whom you see week in and week out. God works through others to shower us with loving kindness and help us through difficult times.

Prayers others may be added

To the Lord who carries our burdens, let us pray, saying:

- **Lord, hear us.**

That the Church may reach out to the poor and the afflicted with the love of Christ, we pray: ▪ That those who carry heavy burdens of depression or addiction may find freedom in Christ, we pray: ▪ That we give glory and honor to Christ in how we receive those reaching out to us in need, especially those with whom we share this ministry of music, we pray: ▪ That those who have died may rejoice in Christ's presence forever, we pray: ▪

Our Father . . .

Lord Jesus Christ,
you bear our burdens.
May we be strong and faithful in all of the trials and afflictions that come to us, knowing that you are with us, to be our strength and support all along the way.
You live and reign for ever and ever. Amen.

Psalm 145:1–2, 8–9, 10–11, 13–14 (see 1)
R. I will praise your name for ever, my king and my God. R/.
OR: R. Alleluia. R/.

† *In the name of the Father, and of the Son, and of the Holy Spirit. Amen.*

† *In the name of the Father, and of the Son, and of the Holy Spirit. Amen.*

Psalm
65:10, 11, 12–13, 14 (Luke 8:8)

R. The seed that falls on good ground will yield a fruitful harvest. R/.

Gospel
Matthew 13:1–9

On that day, Jesus went out of the house and sat down by the sea. Such large crowds gathered around him that he got into a boat and sat down, and the whole crowd stood along the shore. And he spoke to them at length in parables, saying: "A sower went out to sow. And as he sowed, some seed fell on the path, and birds came and ate it up. Some fell on rocky ground, where it had little soil. It sprang up at once because the soil was not deep, and when the sun rose it was scorched, and it withered for lack of roots. Some seed fell among thorns, and the thorns grew up and choked it. But some seed fell on rich soil and produced fruit, a hundred or sixty or thirtyfold. Whoever has ears ought to hear."

Silent Reflection

It is perhaps too obvious to compare the good seed of diligent rehearsal with the seed that fell on rich soil and produced fruit a hundred or sixty or thirtyfold. Still, there is no denying that faithful practice over time produces the desired sound from the choir. Saying yes to this ministry assumes a responsibility, temporary or unexpected absences aside, to be present

every week at rehearsal. Be the good soil from which can come the best fruit. This is the fruit that the assembly needs.

Prayers
others may be added

To the Master of the harvest, we pray, saying:

▪ **Lord, hear us.**

That the Church may spread the good seed of God's Word far and wide, we pray: ▪ That all who have heard the Word of God may bear fruit that will remain, we pray: ▪ That those who struggle to believe may come to know God's love for them, we pray: ▪ That those who have died, marked with the sign of faith, may rise to new life in Christ, we pray: ▪ That we grow in our commitment to the faithful service of our ministry, we pray: ▪

Our Father . . .

*Lord God,
you are the seed and the sower; you are the Master of the harvest.
May the Word you share with us so abundantly take root in us and bring forth an abundant harvest in words and deeds of love.
We ask this through Christ our Lord.
Amen.*

Psalm
65:10, 11, 12–13, 14 (Luke 8:8)

R. The seed that falls on good ground will yield a fruitful harvest. R/.

† *In the name of the Father, and of the Son, and of the Holy Spirit. Amen.*

† *In the name of the Father, and of the Son, and of the Holy Spirit. Amen.*

Psalm
86:5–6, 9–10, 15–16 (5a)

R. Lord, you are good and forgiving. R/.

Gospel
Matthew 13:24–30

Jesus proposed another parable to the crowds, saying: "The kingdom of heaven may be likened to a man who sowed good seed in his field. While everyone was asleep his enemy came and sowed weeds all through the wheat, and then went off. When the crop grew and bore fruit, the weeds appeared as well. The slaves of the householder came to him and said, 'Master, did you not sow good seed in your field? Where have the weeds come from?' He answered, 'An enemy has done this.' His slaves said to him, 'Do you want us to go and pull them up?' He replied, 'No, if you pull up the weeds you might uproot the wheat along with them. Let them grow together until harvest; then at harvest time I will say to the harvesters, "First collect the weeds and tie them in bundles for burning; but gather the wheat into my barn."'"

Silent Reflection

We have within us any number of sub-personalities, some that help us and some that sabotage, like the good seed and the weeds growing side by side. One saboteur can be that part of us that repeatedly gives in to unhealthy eating, poor sleeping habits, smoking, or whatever else might seem worth it in the moment but in the long run effects the health of our voice or our entire body. Without judging, dare to acknowledge these "weeds within" that hinder being your best voice in the choir. Then focus on whatever part of you has the courage to make a change.

Prayers
others may be added

To the Master of the harvest, we pray, saying:

▪ **Lord, hear our prayer.**

That the Church may sow the good seed of the Gospel in every place, until the end of time, we pray: ▪ That lawyers and judges may be just and fair in all of their dealings, we pray: ▪ That choir members are challenging yet gentle with themselves as they strive to care for the instruments of their voices, we pray: ▪ That those who have died believing in Christ's mercy may find in him a merciful judge, we pray: ▪

Our Father . . .

Lord God,
it is so easy to judge, so difficult to forgive.
Free us from our need to judge others,
and guide us in your mysterious way
of love.
We ask this through Christ our Lord.
Amen.

Psalm
86:5–6, 9–10, 15–16 (5a)

R. Lord, you are good and forgiving. R/.

† *In the name of the Father, and of the Son, and of the Holy Spirit. Amen.*

† *In the name of the Father, and of the Son, and of the Holy Spirit. Amen.*

Psalm
119:57, 72, 76–77, 127–128, 129–130 (97a)

R. Lord, I love your commands. R/.

Gospel
Matthew 13:44–52

[Jesus said to the disciples:] "The kingdom of heaven is like a net thrown into the sea, which collects fish of every kind. When it is full they haul it ashore and sit down to put what is good into buckets. What is bad they throw away. Thus it will be at the end of the age. The angels will go out and separate the wicked from the righteous and throw them into the fiery furnace, where there will be wailing and grinding of teeth."

Silent Reflection

In the world of those who fish, the ones thrown back are usually the ones that are too small. The ones kept for eating are the good ones. The others are bad for now, but may yet grow enough to be used for food. Would you say you can still grow in your ministry as a choir member? How about more growth as a Christian? Sometimes we practice outside of regular rehearsals, by ourselves or with a few others, in order to improve how we render the music. What are ways in which you seek growth in your understanding of who you are as a follower of Christ?

Prayers
others may be added

To the God who promises his Kingdom to the peacemakers, let us pray, saying:

▪ **Thy Kingdom come.**

That the Church may establish God's Kingdom on earth by doing as Jesus taught, we pray: ▪ That those who are beginning to know God may seek him in all things and above all things, we pray: ▪ That those who lack the basic necessities of life may have the help they need, we pray: ▪ That those who have died in Christ may know the reward promised to good and faithful servants, we pray: ▪ That as we strive to be more artful in our music-making, so may we never cease to expand our consciousness toward greater unity with Christ, we pray: ▪

Our Father . . .

Lord God, we long for your presence; increase our longing and fill our hearts with love of you, so that we may seek your Kingdom with all of our strength and know the joy of those who have obtained the pearl of great price. We ask this through Christ our Lord. Amen.

Psalm
119:57, 72, 76–77, 127–128, 129–130 (97a)

R. Lord, I love your commands. R/.

† *In the name of the Father, and of the Son, and of the Holy Spirit. Amen.*

August 3, 2014
Eighteenth Sunday in Ordinary Time

† In the name of the Father, and of the Son, and of the Holy Spirit. Amen.

Psalm
145:8–9, 15–16, 17–18 (see 16)

R. The hand of the Lord feeds us; he answers all our needs. R/.

Gospel
Matthew 14:15–20

When it was evening, the disciples approached [Jesus] and said, "This is a deserted place and it is already late; dismiss the crowds so that they can go to the villages and buy food for themselves." Jesus said to them, "There is no need for them to go away; give them some food yourselves." But they said to him, "Five loaves and two fish are all we have here." Then he said, "Bring them here to me," and he ordered the crowds to sit down on the grass. Taking the five loaves and the two fish, and looking up to heaven, he said the blessing, broke the loaves, and gave them to the disciples, who in turn gave them to the crowds. They all ate and were satisfied.

Silent Reflection

Each day brings us opportunities to be magnanimous in relating with others, to assure that in any situation everyone is served in some way. Take notice of these opportunities at home, in your work place, at play, at choir practice—wherever it is that need arises. The Gospel says *all* were fed. Honor your own need even as you look for a way to cooperate so that all can be satisfied. What can you offer toward bringing this about? Within the choir as well as in other parts of life, this will contribute to greater harmony.

Prayers
others may be added

To the God who spreads a table before us, let us pray, saying:

▪ **Lord, hear our prayer.**

That the Church, sustained by the Eucharist, may invite all to the banquet of life, we pray: ▪ That those who suffer malnutrition and hunger in our world may receive a share of the earth's bounty, we pray: ▪ That those who hunger and thirst for justice may be satisfied, we pray: ▪ That within our choir community we practice balancing the needs of others along with our own so as to grow in the habit of fostering happiness and peace, we pray: ▪

Our Father . . .

Lord our God,
joy, hope, love, abundance: these are
     the signs of your presence.
May we be aware that you are with us
     and give thanks for your bounty
     and goodness.
We ask this through Christ our Lord.
Amen.

Psalm
145:8–9, 15–16, 17–18 (see 16)

R. The hand of the Lord feeds us; he answers all our needs. R/.

† In the name of the Father, and of the Son, and of the Holy Spirit. Amen.

† *In the name of the Father, and of the Son, and of the Holy Spirit. Amen.*

Psalm
85:9, 10, 11–12, 13–14 (8)

R. Lord, let us see your kindness, and grant us your salvation. R/.

Gospel
Matthew 14:22–33

When the disciples saw [Jesus] walking on the sea they were terrified. "It is a ghost," they said, and they cried out in fear. At once Jesus spoke to them, "Take courage, it is I; do not be afraid." Peter said to him in reply, "Lord, if it is you, command me to come to you on the water." He said, "Come." Peter got out of the boat and began to walk on the water toward Jesus. But when he saw how strong the wind was he became frightened; and, beginning to sink, he cried out, "Lord, save me!" Immediately Jesus stretched out his hand and caught him, and said to him, "O you of little faith, why did you doubt?" After they got into the boat, the wind died down. Those who were in the boat did him homage, saying, "Truly, you are the Son of God."

Silent Reflection

How many times do we doubt, mistrust, fall short, or give up in spite of the countless memories we have of successes, or of making it through a difficulty? Even the presence of Jesus didn't sustain Peter and help him hold onto the trust that surged initially. Have you ever said, like you might about a piece of music, "I'll never get this"? When we suspend doubt in small ways and then succeed, like we do when we learn that difficult song, we practice letting go and trusting. Facing larger life issues, we are better able to surrender to their mystery and know God is with us.

Prayers
others may be added

Trusting in the Lord's power to save, we pray:

▪ **We believe, Lord; help our unbelief.**

That the Church may look to the future with hope, knowing that Christ will always be with us, we pray: ▪ That those who are working to establish peace and justice in the world may never lose heart, we pray: ▪ That those who are experiencing trials may hold fast to the Lord Jesus, we pray: ▪ That whether in our home, in our parish, in our neighborhoods, or in our rehearsals, we keep our hearts focused on God's love and abiding presence always and in everything, we pray: ▪

Our Father . . .

Lord God,
keep us from the fear that cripples us,
that keeps us from venturing forth in new directions.
Let us hear the voice of your Son, saying to us, "Courage. Do not be afraid."
We ask this through the same Christ our Lord.
Amen.

Psalm
85:9, 10, 11–12, 13–14 (8)

R. Lord, let us see your kindness, and grant us your salvation. R/.

† *In the name of the Father, and of the Son, and of the Holy Spirit. Amen.*

† *In the name of the Father, and of the Son, and of the Holy Spirit. Amen.*

Psalm
45:10, 11, 12, 16 (10bc)

R. The queen stands at your right hand, arrayed in gold. R/.

Gospel
Luke 11:27–28

While Jesus was speaking, a woman from the crowd called out and said to him, "Blessed is the womb that carried you and the breasts at which you nursed." He replied, "Rather, blessed are those who hear the word of God and observe it."

Silent Reflection

When you reflect upon your life, what moments stand out? For what memories are you most grateful? Be sure to include what the gift of music has given you. Savor *all* of what comes; breathe deeply of the life you have, of all that life has brought you to now. None of it would be if not for the mother who brought you into the world. With gratitude, we bless our mothers as we bless Mary, Mother of God. Even more, we embody our thanksgiving by being life-givers ourselves, giving birth to the Word of God alive in us, bringing it forth into the world.

Prayers
others may be added

With the prayers of Mary, taken up into heaven, to help us, we pray:

▪ **Lord, hear our prayer.**

That Mary, Mother of the Church, may intercede for all the baptized, we pray: ▪ That there may be peace in the world and in every human heart, we pray: ▪ That our beloved dead may come into God's presence, with all their sins forgiven, we pray: ▪ That our songs and our very lives will inspire others to grow to a fullness of life in the spirit, we pray: ▪ That we may pattern our lives on the faith and obedience of the Blessed Virgin Mary, we pray: ▪

Our Father . . .

Lord our God,
you have given us the Blessed Virgin
Mary to be our mother, our queen,
and our model of discipleship.
May we follow Christ as she did, in
simplicity, faithfulness, and love,
until we are united with him
in heaven.
Grant this through the same Christ
our Lord.
Amen.

Psalm
45:10, 11, 12, 16 (10bc)

R. The queen stands at your right hand, arrayed in gold. R/.

† *In the name of the Father, and of the Son, and of the Holy Spirit. Amen.*

† *In the name of the Father, and of the Son, and of the Holy Spirit. Amen.*

Psalm
67:2–3, 5, 6, 8 (4)

R. O God, let all the nations praise you! R/.

Gospel
Matthew 15:21–28

At that time Jesus withdrew to the region of Tyre and Sidon. And behold, a Canaanite woman of that district came and called out, "Have pity on me, Lord, Son of David! My daughter is tormented by a demon." But he did not say a word in answer to her. Jesus' disciples came and asked him, "Send her away, for she keeps calling out after us." He said in reply, "I was sent only to the lost sheep of the house of Israel." But the woman came and did him homage, saying, "Lord, help me." He said in reply, "It is not right to take the food of the children and throw it to the dogs." She said, "Please, Lord, for even the dogs eat the scraps that fall from the table of their masters." Then Jesus said to her in reply, "O woman, great is your faith! Let it be done for you as you wish." And her daughter was healed from that hour.

Silent Reflection

She was acting out of love for her daughter, this woman in the Gospel who would not let Jesus go without helping her. Jesus was moved by her faith and it opened him to go beyond what he perceived he was called to do. What is your experience of being called out beyond what you imagined or expected of yourself? Has that ever happened in the context of your ministry in music, perhaps by singing a solo or serving as cantor, or playing the bells or percussion written for a certain piece? What did you learn about yourself? To answer, finish the sentence, "I am. . . ."

Prayers
others may be added

To the God of every nation, let us bring our prayers and praise, saying:

▪ **Lord, hear us.**

For the Church, that we may reach beyond borders to all who stand in need, we pray: ▪ For parents who suffer anguish because of the illness or sin of a child, that they may persevere in prayer like the Canaanite woman, we pray: ▪ For the wisdom to go beyond initial perceptions of ourselves or others in order to discover, like Jesus finding deep faith in the Canaanite woman, more of the gifts in each of us, we pray: ▪

Our Father . . .

Lord our God,
there are no outsiders in your Kingdom,
for your love reaches beyond
all boundaries.
May we learn to love others as you
love them.
We ask this through Christ our Lord.
Amen.

Psalm
67:2–3, 5, 6, 8 (4)

R. O God, let all the nations praise you! R/.

† *In the name of the Father, and of the Son, and of the Holy Spirit. Amen.*

August 24, 2014
Twenty-First Sunday in Ordinary Time

† In the name of the Father, and of the Son, and of the Holy Spirit. Amen.

Psalm
138:1–2, 2–3, 6, 8 (8bc)

R. Lord, your love is eternal; do not forsake the work of your hands. R/.

Gospel
Matthew 16:13–20

Jesus went into the region of Caesarea Philippi and he asked his disciples, "Who do people say that the Son of Man is?" They replied, "Some say John the Baptist, others Elijah, still others Jeremiah or one of the prophets." He said to them, "But who do you say that I am?" Simon Peter said in reply, "You are the Christ, the Son of the living God." Jesus said to him in reply, "Blessed are you, Simon son of Jonah. For flesh and blood has not revealed this to you, but my heavenly Father. And so I say to you, you are Peter, and upon this rock I will build my church, and the gates of the netherworld shall not prevail against it. I will give you the keys to the kingdom of heaven. Whatever you bind on earth shall be bound in heaven; and whatever you loose on earth shall be loosed in heaven." Then he strictly ordered his disciples to tell no one that he was the Christ.

Silent Reflection

You have sung so many texts that are directly from Scripture or at least in the spirit of the Christian way of life! For how many weeks, months, and years, have they been taken in, forming you? How much have you perceived their gradual effect on you, changing and reshaping you? Have they heightened your image of the Divine? Of Christ? Take some moments to ponder how you would answer the question posed by Jesus, "Who do you say I am?" You might also share your answer with another, or at least write down your response for yourself, to reflect upon again.

Prayers
others may be added

To the Lord who has words of eternal life, we pray, saying:

▪ **Lord, hear us.**

That the Church, built upon Peter's profession of faith, may withstand every storm, we pray: ▪ That the world may be blessed with true and lasting peace, we pray: ▪ That those who have gone before us, marked with the sign of faith, may rejoice forever in God's Kingdom, we pray: ▪ That we remember to stop and give thanks for how we are evolving in our journey of faith, we pray: ▪

Our Father . . .

Lord Jesus Christ,
Son of the living God, increase our faith,
until our knowledge of you echoes
in everything we say and everything
we do.
You live and reign for ever and ever.
Amen.

Psalm
138:1–2, 2–3, 6, 8 (8bc)

R. Lord, your love is eternal; do not forsake the work of your hands. R/.

† In the name of the Father, and of the Son, and of the Holy Spirit. Amen.

August 31, 2014
Twenty-Second Sunday in Ordinary Time

† In the name of the Father, and of the Son, and of the Holy Spirit. Amen.

Psalm
63:2, 3–4, 5–6, 8–9 (2b)

R. My soul is thirsting for you, O Lord my God. R/.

Gospel
Matthew 16:24–27

Jesus said to his disciples, "Whoever wishes to come after me must deny himself, take up his cross, and follow me. For whoever wishes to save his life will lose it, but whoever loses his life for my sake will find it. What profit would there be for one to gain the whole world and forfeit his life? Or what can one give in exchange for his life? For the Son of Man will come with his angels in his Father's glory, and then he will repay everyone according to his conduct."

Silent Reflection

We are called to embrace the paradox of Paschal Mystery—Death and Resurrection, losing our life to find it. Crosses in life come to all. Each of us suffers at different times and in different ways. We see this over and over in our own lives, in the news, and in the experiences of the people in the small community of our choir. Do we hold a cross in bitterness or hold it with the hope of transformation? It matters how we enter into this Mystery. The more we surrender, the greater our witness to trust in God. This, too, is our work as ministers, as faithful servants.

Prayers
others may be added

In the name of Christ, who suffered on the Cross for us, let us pray, saying:

▪ **Lord, by your Cross and Resurrection you have set us free.**

That all Christians may joyfully accept a share in Christ's Cross, and come to eternal life with him, we pray: ▪ That we may reach out with love and generosity to those suffering the ravages of hunger and disease, we pray: ▪ That our beloved dead may stand before the throne of God, with all of their sins forgiven, we pray: ▪ That in willingly taking up our cross we will deepen in faith and be strengthened as ministers of the sung Word, we pray: ▪

Our Father . . .

Lord Jesus Christ,
you teach us to take up our cross
and follow.
Help us to recognize the crosses in our
daily lives,
and instead of stumbling over them,
take them up with courage
and follow after you.
You who live and reign with the Father
and the Holy Spirit,
one God, for ever and ever.
Amen.

Psalm
63:2, 3–4, 5–6, 8–9 (2b)

R. My soul is thirsting for you, O Lord my God. R/.

† In the name of the Father, and of the Son, and of the Holy Spirit. Amen.

September 7, 2014
Twenty-Third Sunday in Ordinary Time

† *In the name of the Father, and of the Son, and of the Holy Spirit. Amen.*

Psalm
95:1–2, 6–7, 8–9 (8)

R. If today you hear his voice, harden not your hearts. R/.

Gospel
Matthew 18:15–17

Jesus said to his disciples: "If your brother sins against you, go and tell him his fault between you and him alone. If he listens to you, you have won over your brother. If he does not listen, take one or two others along with you, so that 'every fact may be established on the testimony of two or three witnesses.' If he refuses to listen to them, tell the church. If he refuses to listen even to the church, then treat him as you would a Gentile or a tax collector."

Silent Reflection

Being with one another week in and week out at rehearsals and at worship can bring about familiarity. Sometimes becoming comfortable with one another can mean we inadvertently say things or do things that are hurtful. Gone is the guardedness or formality we bring to other situations that perhaps helps us pay more attention to our words and actions. The Gospel story implores us to talk about such things rather than let them be a wedge between us. We must also be open to acknowledging any hurt we have done, even if unintended, and ask for forgiveness.

Prayers
others may be added

Knowing that Christ is with us in our prayer, we pray:

▪ **Lord, hear us.**

That the Church may welcome sinners as Christ welcomed them, we pray: ▪ That the leaders of nations may not hesitate to undertake the difficult work of building peace, we pray: ▪ That all who are hearing the call to discipleship may follow God without fear, we pray: ▪ That we may recognize and act upon our awareness that our growing closer as a community of musicians is vital to the music we make, we pray: ▪

Our Father . . .

Lord Jesus Christ,
you have taught us to be gentle with
each other, loving and forgiving
each other.
May our families and our parishes be
one in love, and may we know your
presence in our midst whenever we
gather for prayer.
You live and reign for ever and ever.
Amen.

Psalm
95:1–2, 6–7, 8–9 (8)

R. If today you hear his voice, harden not your hearts. R/.

† *In the name of the Father, and of the Son, and of the Holy Spirit. Amen.*

September 14, 2014
Feast of the Exaltation of the Holy Cross

† In the name of the Father, and of the Son, and of the Holy Spirit. Amen.

Psalm   78:1–2, 34–35, 36–37, 38 (see 7b)
R. Do not forget the works of the Lord! R/.

Gospel   John 3:13–17

Jesus said to Nicodemus: "No one has gone up to heaven except the one who has come down from heaven, the Son of Man. And just as Moses lifted up the serpent in the desert, so must the Son of Man be lifted up, so that everyone who believes in him may have eternal life."

For God so loved the world that he gave his only Son, so that everyone who believes in him might not perish but might have eternal life. For God did not send his Son into the world to condemn the world, but that the world might be saved through him.

Silent Reflection

Many parishes gather to pray monthly in the spirit of Taizé, a Christian ecumenical prayer. A ritual that is sometimes a part of this prayer is called Prayer Around the Cross. Different from the Veneration of the Cross on Good Friday, this is an opportunity to bring our burdens and cares (or those we know others carry) to the Cross, to mark how we are not alone with them. During this ritual there is much singing, although there is usually no formal choir. For choir members, this can be a time of renewal, of allowing others in the assembly to minister to you.

Prayers   others may be added

We glory in the Cross of our Lord Jesus Christ, and so we pray:

▪ Save us through your Cross, O Lord.

That the baptized may look to the Cross of Christ for the promise of eternal life, we pray: ▪ That leaders of nations may work together to protect all human life, we pray: ▪ That all who suffer may see in their sufferings a share in Christ's glorious Cross, we pray: ▪ That as ministers we honor the loving sacrifice of Christ not only by how we give of ourselves, but also how we humble ourselves to receive from others, we pray: ▪

Our Father . . .

Lord our God,
we glory in the Cross of our Lord
     Jesus Christ.
May we learn to glory in the sufferings of
     our lives, for the same power which
     transformed the Cross into the Tree
     of Life can transform our sufferings
     into joy and grace.
We pray through Christ our Lord.
Amen.

Psalm   78:1–2, 34–35, 36–37, 38 (see 7b)
R. Do not forget the works of the Lord! R/.

† In the name of the Father, and of the Son, and of the Holy Spirit. Amen.

September 21, 2014
Twenty-Fifth Sunday in Ordinary Time

† *In the name of the Father, and of the Son, and of the Holy Spirit. Amen.*

Psalm
145:2–3, 8–9, 17–18 (18a)

R. The Lord is near to all who call upon him. R/.

Gospel
Matthew 20:8–16

"When it was evening the owner of the vineyard said to his foreman, 'Summon the laborers and give them their pay, beginning with the last and ending with the first.' When those who had started about five o'clock came, each received the usual daily wage. So when the first came, they thought that they would receive more, but each of them also got the usual wage. And on receiving it they grumbled against the landowner, saying, 'These last ones worked only one hour, and you have made them equal to us, who bore the day's burden and the heat.' He said to one of them in reply, 'My friend, I am not cheating you. Did you not agree with me for the usual daily wage? Take what is yours and go. What if I wish to give this last one the same as you? Or am I not free to do as I wish with my own money? Are you envious because I am generous?' Thus, the last will be first, and the first will be last."

Silent Reflection

Applied to the choir, might the Gospel be interpreted as saying there is no place for judgment or for an attitude of entitlement? How does it address those times when we grumble or delight about being placed in a certain section, or being singled out for a solo? Perhaps something the music director can take from this Scripture is the challenge to be worthy of trust, to make just choices, and to be upfront and clear with expectations. May we each do our part to foster generosity in our relationships and unconditional joy in the work of our music ministry.

Prayers
others may be added

Trusting in the generosity of God, we pray:

▪ **Lord, hear our prayer.**

For the Church, that all the faithful may work for the coming of the Kingdom, we pray: ▪ For the world, that the wealthy nations of the world may share their plenty with those who are struggling, we pray: ▪ That we may give freely and lovingly of ourselves in our ministry and in all we do, not counting the cost, we pray: ▪

Our Father . . .

*Lord our God,
you have called us to labor in your
    vineyard.
May we work faithfully until the end, and
    receive the reward of our labors.
We ask this through Christ our Lord.
Amen.*

Psalm
145:2–3, 8–9, 17–18 (18a)

R. The Lord is near to all who call upon him. R/.

† *In the name of the Father, and of the Son, and of the Holy Spirit. Amen.*

September 28, 2014
Twenty-Sixth Sunday in Ordinary Time

† *In the name of the Father, and of the Son, and of the Holy Spirit. Amen.*

Psalm
25:4–5, 6–7, 8–9 (6a)

R. Remember your mercies, O Lord. R/.

Gospel
Matthew 21:28–31

Jesus said to the chief priests and elders of the people: "What is your opinion? A man had two sons. He came to the first and said, 'Son, go out and work in the vineyard today.' He said in reply, 'I will not,' but afterwards changed his mind and went. The man came to the other son and gave the same order. He said in reply, 'Yes, sir,' but did not go. Which of the two did his father's will?" They answered, "The first." Jesus said to them, "Amen, I say to you, tax collectors and prostitutes are entering the kingdom of God before you."

Silent Reflection

Sometimes it takes time to catch up with whatever is truest in us. So, we may say no to a request and then turn around and act upon it anyway. Or, we may say yes without thinking through something and then neglect it or ignore it entirely. Perhaps it's best to delay a response until taking time to go inside and discovering if whatever is being asked is something you can fulfill, so that your inward and outward responses are in tune. Occasionally bring this practice of mindfulness to your "yes" in music ministry. Is the call still there, or are you being called to something else?

Prayers
others may be added

To the God who calls us to do his will, we pray:

▪ **Lord, have mercy.**

That the leaders of the Church may always seek to do God's will in good times and bad, we pray: ▪ That those who lack the basic necessities of life may receive what they need, we pray: ▪ That we may recognize the poor in our midst and reach out to them, we pray: ▪ That we may do the will of God, not in words alone, but in actions, we pray: ▪

Our Father . . .

Lord our God,
we have made many promises
to you; how many times have
we broken them?
Give us the grace of true repentance, and
the strength to walk in your ways,
doing all that you have asked of us.
We ask this through Christ our Lord.
Amen.

Psalm
25:4–5, 6–7, 8–9 (6a)

R. Remember your mercies, O Lord. R/.

† *In the name of the Father, and of the Son, and of the Holy Spirit. Amen.*

October 5, 2014

Twenty-Seventh Sunday in Ordinary Time

† *In the name of the Father, and of the Son, and of the Holy Spirit. Amen.*

Psalm
80:9, 12, 13–14, 15–16, 19–20
(Isaiah 5:7a)

R. The vineyard of the Lord is the house of Israel. R/.

Gospel
Matthew 21:33–39a, 43

"There was a landowner who planted a vineyard, put a hedge around it, dug a wine press in it, and built a tower. Then he leased it to tenants and went on a journey. When vintage time drew near, he sent his servants to the tenants to obtain his produce. But the tenants seized the servants and one they beat, another they killed, and a third they stoned. Again he sent other servants, more numerous than the first ones, but they treated them in the same way. Finally, he sent his son to them, thinking, 'They will respect my son.' But when the tenants saw the son, they said to one another, 'This is the heir. Come, let us kill him and acquire his inheritance.' They seized him, threw him out of the vineyard and killed him. . . . Therefore, I say to you, the kingdom of God will be taken away from you and given to a people that will produce its fruit."

Silent Reflection

What if we looked upon our singing voices as the vineyards and God as the landowner? What kind of tenants are we? Are we caring for our "vineyards"? In other words, how much energy do we give to maintaining good vocal health? For instance, besides being on time for the vocal warm-ups before Mass or rehearsal, might we try doing them more often on our own? How do we guard against over-extending or over-using our voices? Does the care we give to our voices honor the gift of them? Be intentional with their treatment.

Prayers
others may be added

To the God who has entrusted us with his priceless gifts, we pray:

▪ **Lord, hear our prayer.**

That the leaders of the Church may be models of humble service of those in need, we pray: ▪ That leaders of nations may not lord it over others, but serve the needs of all, we pray: ▪ That we may recognize the voices of all the prophets who come our way, we pray: ▪ That we may do all we can to treasure and respect God's gift of our singing voices and use them to bring forth beauty, we pray: ▪

Our Father . . .

Lord God,
make us good stewards of all you have entrusted to us.
Mindful of your Son's coming, may we welcome wisdom and labor in the vineyard with zeal and hope.
We ask this through Christ our Lord. Amen.

Psalm
80:9, 12, 13–14, 15–16, 19–20
(Isaiah 5:7a)

R. The vineyard of the Lord is the house of Israel. R/.

† *In the name of the Father, and of the Son, and of the Holy Spirit. Amen.*

† In the name of the Father, and of the Son, and of the Holy Spirit. Amen.

Psalm
23:1–3a, 3b–4, 5, 6 (6cd)

R. I shall live in the house of the Lord all the days of my life. R/.

Gospel
Matthew 22:1b–9

[Jesus said:] "The kingdom of heaven may be likened to a king who gave a wedding feast for his son. He dispatched his servants to summon the invited guests to the feast, but they refused to come. A second time he sent other servants, saying, 'Tell those invited: "Behold, I have prepared my banquet, my calves and fattened cattle are killed and everything is ready; come to the feast." ' Some ignored the invitation and went away, one to his farm, another to his business. The rest laid hold of his servants, mistreated them, and killed them. The king was enraged and sent his troops, destroyed those murderers, and burned their city. Then the king said to his servants, 'The feast is ready, but those who were invited were not worthy to come. Go out, therefore, into the main roads and invite to the feast whomever you find.'"

Silent Reflection

In our music, in our song, we extend an invitation to those who are assembled to unite with us. The passion of our invitation comes from knowing its intimacy, that whether in praise, thanksgiving, joy, or supplication, song draws us more deeply into communion with Divine Mystery. We cannot control how, when, or even if the invitation is received. It is for us to remain faithful to the work entrusted to us and then to let go, trusting in God's faithfulness, love, and grace.

Prayers
others may be added

To the Lord of heaven and earth, we pray:

▪ **Lord, hear our prayer.**

For the holy Church of God, that we may find unity in the midst of diversity, we pray: ▪ For our families, communities, and friends, that we may be drawn together in love, we pray: ▪ For pastoral musicians, that we may be worthy of our ministry, offered in love to the worshipping community, we pray: ▪ For those who have died, that they may come to the banquet of heaven, we pray: ▪

Our Father . . .

Lord our God,
you have called us
to the marriage-supper of the Lamb.
May we come to the feast
with open hearts,
clothed in Christ
and ready to do your will.
We ask this through Christ our Lord.
Amen.

Psalm
23:1–3a, 3b–4, 5, 6 (6cd)

R. I shall live in the house of the Lord all the days of my life. R/.

† In the name of the Father, and of the Son, and of the Holy Spirit. Amen.

October 19, 2014
Twenty-Ninth Sunday in Ordinary Time

† *In the name of the Father, and of the Son, and of the Holy Spirit. Amen.*

Psalm
96:1, 3, 4–5, 7–8, 9–10 (7b)

R. Give the Lord glory and honor. R/.

Gospel
Matthew 22:15, 17–21

The Pharisees . . . plotted how they might entrap Jesus in speech, . . . saying, . . . "Tell us, then, what is your opinion: Is it lawful to pay the census tax to Caesar or not?" Knowing their malice, Jesus said, "Why are you testing me, you hypocrites? Show me the coin that pays the census tax." Then they handed him the Roman coin. He said to them, "Whose image is this and whose inscription?" They replied, "Caesar's." At that he said to them, "Then repay to Caesar what belongs to Caesar and to God what belongs to God."

Silent Reflection

There are those who cannot be a part of the parish choir because they find it too difficult to commit to the weekly rehearsal schedule. Work, family, or other situations must be given priority. These are people for whom occasional choirs, for which the rehearsal schedule is less demanding, can provide an answer. What would it take for a parish music program to widen its opportunities for service, like with a men's choir for Good Friday, a family choir during summer months, a funeral choir, or in some other creative way? Be open to wherever the question leads.

Prayers
others may be added

To the Lord who hears the prayers of all who call on him, we pray:

▪ **Lord, graciously hear us.**

That the Church may bring the teachings of the Gospel to light with gentleness and persistence, we pray: ▪ That those who are yearning for justice may not lose hope, we pray: ▪ That, as a music community, we may be open to exploring together and helping bring to reality new possibilities for the inclusion of those who desire to share their musical gifts, we pray: ▪ That all in authority over others may be models of justice and kindness, we pray: ▪ That we may render unto God the things that are God's, we pray: ▪

Our Father . . .

Lord our God,
fill us with your wisdom, so that we may be good citizens of this world and never forget that our true citizenship is in heaven.
We ask this through Christ our Lord. Amen.

Psalm
96:1, 3, 4–5, 7–8, 9–10 (7b)

R. Give the Lord glory and honor. R/.

† *In the name of the Father, and of the Son, and of the Holy Spirit. Amen.*

October 26, 2014

Thirtieth Sunday in Ordinary Time

† In the name of the Father, and of the Son, and of the Holy Spirit. Amen.

Psalm
18:2–3, 3–4, 47, 51 (2)

R. I love you, Lord, my strength. R/.

Gospel
Matthew 22:34–40

When the Pharisees heard that Jesus had silenced the Sadducees, they gathered together, and one of them a scholar of the law, tested him by asking, "Teacher, which commandment in the law is the greatest?" Jesus said to him, "You shall love the Lord, your God, with all your heart, with all your soul, and with all your mind. This is the greatest and the first commandment. The second is like it: You shall love your neighbor as yourself. The whole law and the prophets depend on these two commandments."

Silent Reflection

There are many ways, big and small, in which we live out these two greatest commandments. Sometimes we don't even think about little gestures as acts of love; we just do them. Yet, every piece of music collected in a timely way after its use and put into the appropriate pile, every bit of help given to get the music filed, every offer of assistance with moving chairs or music stands or keeping the music area clean, is an act of love. What may be missing is the mindfulness of doing each task with this intention. It just takes a moment to bring up this focus.

Prayers
others may be added

With longing for the coming of God's Kingdom, we pray:

▪ **Lord, hear our prayer.**

That the Church may build communities of peace and hope, we pray: ▪ That all who long for peace may work for justice, we pray: ▪ That all our beloved dead may be brought into God's Kingdom of love and light, we pray: ▪ That we may recognize in the way we relieve the burdens of others, like our music director, our desire to love as Jesus taught and lived, we pray: ▪ That we may help to prepare the world for the coming of the Kingdom by our deeds of love, we pray: ▪

Our Father . . .

Lord our God,
we long for a community where we can
trust each other, rely on each other,
and bear one another's burdens.
May we begin to build that community
today by the way we live.
We ask this through Christ our Lord.
Amen.

Psalm
18:2–3, 3–4, 47, 51 (2)

R. I love you, Lord, my strength. R/.

† In the name of the Father, and of the Son, and of the Holy Spirit. Amen.

November 2, 2014

The Commemoration of All the Faithful Departed
(All Souls' Day)

† *In the name of the Father, and of the Son, and of the Holy Spirit. Amen.*

Psalm *23:1–3a, 3b–4, 5, 6 (1) (4ab)*

R. The Lord is my shepherd; there is nothing I shall want. R/.

OR: R. Though I walk in the valley of darkness, I fear no evil, for you are with me. R/.

Gospel *John 6:37–40*

Jesus said to the crowds, "Everything that the Father gives me will come to me, and I will not reject anyone who comes to me, because I came down from heaven not to do my own will but the will of the one who sent me. And this is the will of the one who sent me, that I should not lose anything of what he gave me, but that I should raise it on the last day. For this is the will of my Father, that everyone who sees the Son and believes in him may have eternal life, and I shall raise him on the last day."

Silent Reflection

In the month of November, many parishes provide a table or altar space on which to place pictures of our beloved dead. There may be deceased members of the choir included among these, or family and friends of the choir members. Whether or not we have a direct connection with these lives, it is good to stop and remember that we are all one in the suffering of loss. Let this awareness affect us to such an extent that a deep compassion flows through our song, bringing healing and comfort to one another and those we serve.

Prayers *others may be added*

To the God of life, let us pray that he may bestow the gift of eternal life on all who have gone before us in faith. And so we pray:

▪ **God of life, hear us.**

That the Church may witness in every nation and every age to Christ's victory over death, we pray: ▪ That all who mourn the dead may know Christ's gifts of hope and peace, we pray: ▪ That in our music as in our lives we give witness to our belief in eternal life, we pray: ▪ That the souls of all the faithful departed may rest in the eternal embrace of the God who loves them, we pray: ▪

Our Father . . .

Lord our God,
source of life and salvation, font of healing and forgiveness, hear the prayers we offer for the dead.
Forgive their sins and raise them to life in your Kingdom, to rejoice with all the saints for ever.
We ask this through Christ our Lord. Amen.

Psalm *23:1–3a, 3b–4, 5, 6 (1) (4ab)*

R. The Lord is my shepherd; there is nothing I shall want. R/.

OR: R. Though I walk in the valley of darkness, I fear no evil, for you are with me. R/.

† *In the name of the Father, and of the Son, and of the Holy Spirit. Amen.*

November 9, 2014

Feast of the Dedication of the Lateran Basilica

† In the name of the Father, and of the Son, and of the Holy Spirit. Amen.

Psalm
46:2–3, 5–6, 8–9 (5)

R. The waters of the river gladden the city of God, the holy dwelling of the Most High. R/.

Gospel
John 2:13–17

Since the Passover of the Jews was near, Jesus went up to Jerusalem. He found in the temple area those who sold oxen, sheep, and doves, as well as the money changers seated there. He made a whip out of cords and drove them all out of the temple area, with the sheep and oxen, and spilled the coins of the money changers and overturned their tables, and to those who sold doves he said, "Take these out of here, and stop making my Father's house a marketplace." His disciples recalled the words of Scripture, *Zeal for your house will consume me.*

Silent Reflection

The Gospel tells us something of Jesus's expectations about God's dwelling place. A holy place is not to be defiled. Yet, is there any part of creation not a part of God's "house"? Isn't all of it holy? Aren't we holy? Given this is true by virtue of God's love and indwelling, let us foster a broad culture of respect. As we make the place of our worship holy in what we do and say there or how we are with one another, and as the choir and musicians add to the reverencing of this "holy ground," let us make such a virtue of respect our "way of being" toward all.

Prayers
others may be added

Together with the Church throughout the world, let us give thanks for God's presence in our midst, as we pray:

▪ Lord, hear our prayer.

For the Church, that she may be cleansed and renewed by the celebration of the sacraments, we pray: ▪ For our Holy Father, that God may fill him with gifts of wisdom, peace, and strength, we pray: ▪ For singers and musicians, that in all we do as ministers and in our daily lives, we mirror to others their holiness, we pray: ▪ For all Christians, that we may be filled with zeal for God's service, we pray: ▪

Our Father . . .

*Lord God,
you have made us one in the Body of Christ, and through our communion in him we have become members of Christ and one another.
Keep your family in unity and peace, and make us worthy to be your dwelling place.
We ask this through Christ our Lord. Amen.*

Psalm
46:2–3, 5–6, 8–9 (5)

R. The waters of the river gladden the city of God, the holy dwelling of the Most High. R/.

† In the name of the Father, and of the Son, and of the Holy Spirit. Amen.

November 16, 2014
Thirty-Third Sunday in Ordinary Time

† *In the name of the Father, and of the Son, and of the Holy Spirit. Amen.*

Psalm
128:1–2, 3, 4–5 (see 1a)

R. Blessed are those who fear the Lord. R/.

Gospel
Matthew 25:14–15, 19–21

Jesus told his disciples this parable: "A man going on a journey called in his servants and entrusted his possessions to them. To one he gave five talents; to another, two; to a third, one—to each according to his ability. Then he went away.

"After a long time the master of those servants came back and settled accounts with them. The one who had received five talents came forward bringing the additional five. He said, 'Master, you gave me five talents. See, I have made five more.' His master said to him, 'Well done, my good and faithful servant. Since you were faithful in small matters, I will give you great responsibilities. Come, share your master's joy.'"

Silent Reflection

Many parishes have a children's choir. Have you, as a music minister, thought about how important you are to these children? You give witness to a way of using well the talents given by God. You manifest a way of fostering a love for music into adulthood. You model faithful service to the parish community. You inspire the desire for excellence, for creating beauty. You may never know what this means to an individual child. Yet, we know that children are formed by their experiences. What you do helps them form a vision of how they can imagine themselves evolving.

Prayers
others may be added

To God, the giver of gifts, we pray with confidence:

▪ **Lord, hear our prayer.**

For the Church, that she may be ceaselessly renewed by the celebration of the sacraments, we pray: ▪ For the nations, that they may seek and strive after peace, we pray: ▪ For the wisdom to be aware of our responsibility to the young to witness good stewardship of the musical talent given by God, we pray: ▪ For all Christians, that they may be strong in faith, filled with the gifts of the Holy Spirit, we pray: ▪ For the courage and imagination to use our God-given talents for the glory of God, we pray: ▪

Our Father . . .

Lord our God,
every good gift comes from you.
You have made us who we are and have
*   given us all we have so that we may*
*   have what we need to contribute to*
*   the building of your Kingdom.*
Give us vision to see that we have a part,
*   however small, in your great plan.*
We ask this through Christ our Lord.
Amen.

Psalm
128:1–2, 3, 4–5 (see 1a)

R. Blessed are those who fear the Lord. R/.

† *In the name of the Father, and of the Son, and of the Holy Spirit. Amen.*

November 23, 2014
Solemnity of Our Lord Jesus Christ, King of the Universe

† *In the name of the Father, and of the Son, and of the Holy Spirit. Amen.*

Psalm
23:1–2, 2–3, 5–6 (1)

R. The Lord is my shepherd; there is nothing I shall want. R/.

Gospel
Matthew 25:31–36

Jesus said to his disciples: "When the Son of Man comes in his glory, and all the angels with him, he will sit upon his glorious throne, and all the nations will be assembled before him. And he will separate them one from another, as a shepherd separates the sheep from the goats. He will place the sheep on his right and the goats on his left. Then the king will say to those on his right, 'Come, you who are blessed by my Father. . . . For I was hungry and you gave me food, I was thirsty and you gave me drink, a stranger and you welcomed me, naked and you clothed me, ill and you cared for me, in prison and you visited me.'"

Silent Reflection

This is the last Sunday in the cycle of the Church year. Like at the end of the calendar year, this could be a good time to take stock, both as individual members of the choir and as a group. On a personal level, how have you grown spiritually? Collectively, how has the choir developed, both as musicians and as ministers? Have you gone to workshops? Taken retreats? Where do you notice there is room to expand still more? As much as feels comfortable, share about this with one another. In particular, speak to how love is more visible in the day in and day out of your lives.

Prayers
others may be added

To Jesus Christ, our King, we pray:

• **Christ, hear us.**

Be present to our pope, our bishops, and our priests; may they model their lives on the mystery of your Cross, we pray: ▪ Guide earthly kingdoms in the way of your Kingdom, we pray: ▪ Give us the courage never to cease deepening, expanding, and growing as Christians and as ministers of music, we pray: ▪ Teach us to reverence you in the poor, the thirsty, the stranger, the naked, the sick, and the imprisoned, we pray: ▪ Remember us in your Kingdom, and grant that we may see you face to face, we pray: ▪

Our Father . . .

Lord Jesus Christ, King of the Universe, teach us the way of your Kingdom:
> *the way of justice, the way of love, the way of peace.*
You live and reign with the Father and the Holy Spirit, one God, for ever and ever.
Amen.

Psalm
23:1–2, 2–3, 5–6 (1)

R. The Lord is my shepherd; there is nothing I shall want. R/.

† *In the name of the Father, and of the Son, and of the Holy Spirit. Amen.*